THE CIT
LOBBYI

W9-CAL-975

THE

CITIZEN'S GUIDE

TO

LOBBYING

CONGRESS

REVISED AND UPDATED

DONALD E. deKIEFFER

CHICAGO
REVIEW
PRESS

Library of Congress Cataloging-in-Publication Data

DeKieffer, Donald E.
  The citizen's guide to lobbying Congress / Donald E. deKieffer. — Rev.
and updated.
     p. cm.
  Includes bibliographical references and index.
  ISBN-13: 978-1-55652-718-0
  ISBN-10: 1-55652-718-7
  1. Lobbying—United States—Handbooks, manuals, etc. I. Title.

  JK1118.D425 2007
  328.73´078—dc22

                                                    2007012251

Cover design: Sarah Olson
Cover image: Hisham F. Ibrahim / Getty Images
Interior design: Jonathan Hahn

© 2007 by Donald E. deKieffer
All rights reserved
Published by Chicago Review Press, Incorporated
814 North Franklin Street
Chicago, Illinois 60610
ISBN-13: 978-1-55652-718-0
ISBN-10: 1-55652-718-7
Printed in the United States of America
5 4 3 2 1

To Nancy,
for tolerating my
hours in the Black Hole

CONTENTS

Acknowledgments xi

1 *So You Want to Be a Lobbyist* 1
What Is Lobbying? ◆ The History of Lobbying ◆ Laws Regulating Lobbying
◆ Lobbying as a Vital Part of the American Political System

2 *What's the Issue?* 7
Single-Issue Lobbies ◆ Multiple-Issue Lobbies ◆ Identifying the Issue

3 *Homework* 11
Research on the Issue ◆ Know Your Enemies ◆ Know Your Friends ◆ What's
the Law? ◆ Who Are the Players? ◆ The Resource Book

4 *The Action Plan* 21
Press Relations ◆ Congressional Contacts ◆ Letters ◆ Demonstrations
Gimmicks ◆ The Hill Blitz ◆ Other

5 *The Press* 29
Advertising ◆ How to Become Newsworthy ◆ Talking to Reporters: Good
Guys and Bad Guys ◆ What Is "Good Press"? ◆ Whether and When to Say
What—and to Whom ◆ Columnists ◆ The Press Release ◆ Clipping Services
◆ What If They Roast You? ◆ Letters to the Editor

6 *Letters to the Hill* 43
Short and Simple: Ask for Action ◆ Names, Addresses, and Serial Numbers ◆
Form Letters Are Weighed, Not Read ◆ The Fact Sheet ◆ Following Up ◆
E-mail

7 *Demonstrations* 55
Demonstrations or Lobbying? ◆ Invite Celebrity Speakers ◆ Media Relations ◆ Signs and Symbols ◆ Timing ◆ Appeal to Justice ◆ Avoid Zealotry ◆ Dealing with the Police ◆ Community Relations ◆ Logistics

8 *The Congressional Hearing* 63
What Are Congressional Hearings? ◆ How to Have a Congressional Hearing Scheduled ◆ How to Be Invited to Testify at a Congressional Hearing ◆ The Statement ◆ Planting Questions ◆ Answering Questions ◆ Press Coverage ◆ The Record

9 *The* Congressional Record 73
What Is the *Congressional Record?* ◆ How to Be Included in the *Congressional Record* ◆ Reprinting of Remarks

10 *The Staff* 77
Who Are They? What Motivates Them? ◆ Structure of the Congressional Staff System ◆ The Administrative Assistant ◆ The Personal Secretary ◆ The Press Aide ◆ The Legislative Assistant ◆ The Committee Staffs ◆ The Initial Contact ◆ Lunch?

11 *The Congressional Visit* 91
Whom to See ◆ The Summary Sheet ◆ Arranging a Visit ◆ Staff Contact ◆ What to Say and How to Say It ◆ Follow-Up

12 *Allies* 99
Government Agencies ◆ Other Interest Groups ◆ Members of Congress ◆ Endorsements

13 *Money* 105
The Law ◆ Gifts to Congressmen, Senators, and Staffs ◆ Campaign Contributions ◆ Nonpolitical Contributions ◆ When, How, and How Much to Give to Whom ◆ Raising Money ◆ The Fundraiser

14 *Gimmicks* 127

Keep It Relevant to Your Issue ◆ Don't Be Disruptive ◆ Be Visible ◆ Contact the Press ◆ Keep It Cheap ◆ Successful Gimmicks

15 *The Hill Blitz* 133

What Is a Blitz? ◆ Preparation and Appointments ◆ Coordination ◆ The Meeting ◆ Follow-Up

16 *What If Things Go Wrong?* 141

Errors of Fact ◆ Additional Information ◆ Sources ◆ Statistics ◆ Things Go Wrong ◆ Changed Circumstances ◆ Insults and Breaches of Protocol

17 *Do You Need a Professional?* 151

What a Professional Lobbyist Can and Can't Do ◆ How Much Will It Cost? ◆ How to Choose a Professional Lobbyist ◆ Law Firms ◆ Public Relations Firms ◆ Independent Lobbying Firms

18 *The Ten Commandments* 161

1. Know Your Facts and Be Accurate in Expressing Them ◆ 2. Know Your Opposition ◆ 3. Correct Errors Immediately ◆ 4. Plan, Coordinate, and Follow Up on Each Contact ◆ 5. Avoid Zealotry ◆ 6. Cultivate Your Allies; Make Sure They Do Their Part ◆ 7. Know the Legislative Process ◆ 8. Be Frugal with Your Money ◆ 9. Grow Thick Skin ◆ 10. Win

19 *Resources* 165

Seminars ◆ Reference Manuals ◆ Periodicals ◆ Governmental Material ◆ Status of Legislation ◆ Political Blogs ◆ Services ◆ Books on Lobbying

Index 189

ACKNOWLEDGMENTS

The author gratefully acknowledges the assistance of Ingo Esders, one of the best labor lobbyists in Washington; Ryan Hardy, for his research skills; and a gaggle of anonymous kibitzers who provided assistance "on deep background." They know who they are.

1

So You Want to
Be a Lobbyist

"I have come to the conclusion that politics is too serious a matter to be left to the politicians."

—Charles de Gaulle

What Is Lobbying?

Outside of Washington, the business of lobbying is generally equated with all sorts of skulduggery—paper bags full of unmarked bills, a little black book filled with the telephone numbers of women of dubious repute, and twenty years of experience in the "old-boy network" of Washington insiders. A lobbyist is about as highly regarded as a Mafia hit man or a crooked county sheriff. Quite frankly, lobbyists themselves have not done much to improve this image, and some intentionally perpetuate these myths to justify their own existence and discourage do-it-yourselfers. Obviously, this book is not designed for them.

Our Constitution guarantees all citizens the unqualified right to petition their government for redress of grievances and the freedom to state their views without governmental interference. In the broadest sense, anyone who writes a letter to a member of Congress or questions a candidate at a political meeting is a lobbyist. But where does one draw the line between merely exercising a constitutionally guaranteed right and lobbying professionally? Perhaps Justice Potter Stewart's famous comment about pornography—that you may not be able to define it but you know it when you see it—also applies to lobbying.

The History of Lobbying

Ever since human beings organized themselves into communities, the course of government policy has been influenced by lobbyists. Over the centuries, lobbyists have gone by different names; during the American Revolution, nongovernmental organizations known as the Committees of Correspondence had an enormous impact upon the future of the Republic. At times lobbyists have camouflaged their true purpose with official-sounding titles; a grand vizier of the thirteenth century was no less a lobbyist than the president of the National Coal Association is today.

Although every country that is not totally anarchic supports some form of lobbying, it is only in the United States that this political phenomenon has been institutionalized. This is due to two primary factors. The first is the structure of our constitutional system. Perhaps because King George had ignored the opinions of the American colonists—or because, as Alexis de Tocqueville noted, the early Americans had a striking tendency to form associations and pressure groups whenever two or more individuals discovered a shared interest—the authors of the Constitution and the Bill of Rights included at least three provisions that protected the freedom of interest groups to present their causes to the government, thus guaranteeing lobbyists a place in the American political system.

The second factor that encouraged the development of lobbying in the United States was the structure of the government itself. Congressmen—and later senators—were and are popularly elected by their respective constituencies. Although numerous philosophical studies and doctoral theses have been written about the function of members of Congress, the original and enduring reality is that congressmen and senators represent their constituents first; their leadership obligations are secondary.*

Empowered by a political structure keyed to the parochial desires of different constituencies and by constitutional guarantees of freedom of expression, the concept of lobbying took strong and early root in the American political system.

---

*Throughout this book, the terms "congressman," "senator," and "member of Congress" are used in accordance with prevailing Washington parlance. "Congressman" refers specifically to a member of the House of Representatives. Common usage still prefers "congressman" over the gender-neutral "congressperson"; I use the former term in deference to this fact and not, I hope, to signify any sexist tendencies on my own part. "Senator" is, quite obviously, a member of the U.S. Senate. And as used in this book, "member of Congress" is a member of either the House of Representatives or the Senate. Unless specifically indicated to the contrary, references to "member" or "member of Congress" imply that the same lobbying techniques are equally applicable to either side of the Congress.

In the earliest days of the United States, lobbying was practiced primarily at the state level. The very term "lobbying" derived from the practice by which state lobbyists pressed their causes in the corridors outside legislative chambers. Because the federal government at that time concerned itself with fewer issues of direct importance to a majority of Americans, fewer lobbyists worked at the federal level. But federal lobbyists did exist—they pressed claims for federal ship-building contracts, asked to supply goods to government agencies, and argued for the central government to help suppress Indian uprisings. A number of fascinating books have been written on the activities of these early lobbyists; some are listed under "Books on Lobbying" at the end of chapter 19.

As the federal government became more complex, lobbyists became more specialized and sophisticated in their approaches. Until the phenomenal growth of congressional staffs in the early 1960s, lobbyists provided much of the political research for members of Congress and competed with the Congressional Research Service (CRS), a branch of the Library of Congress, to supply background data in support of (or in opposition to) proposed legislation. Although it still seems sacrilegious to those outside the Washington Beltway, lobbyists have actually been writing much of the legislation of this country since its earliest days.

Throughout the eighteenth century and most of the nineteenth, however, the lobbyists' trade was practiced discreetly. There was little public disclosure of their activities and certainly no requirement for registration. This secrecy is partially responsible for the low esteem in which lobbyists generally are held today. "Influence peddling" has a long and sometimes unsavory history, and part of its mystique remains.

The shady underside of the lobbyist's craft was a subject of intense speculation and outright fabrication during the late nineteenth century. Just as dime novels glamorized the American West, newspapers and fiction writers of the time made lobbying the subject of lurid speculation. Exposés of lobbyists for the great capitalist institutions continued well into the twentieth century. Lobbyists were characterized as little better than panderers and blackmailers, suborning public officials for their own greedy ends. Titillating stories were written about the methods used by these scoundrels, which rarely failed to include the use of wine and women to promote their schemes—almost always to the detriment of the Republic.

Public outrage did not come like a thunderclap as in the later case of Watergate, but rather through a growing sense of revulsion at the perceived evils of graft and corruption spawned by lobbyists. Early on, there was talk of banning lobbyists entirely, but even though public outrage had become intense, an outright ban on lobbying faced insurmountable constitutional hurdles.

On the theory that corruption does not flourish in the sunshine, the Congress* did succeed in passing some laws requiring lobbyists to disclose their activities publicly. Timid as these early laws appear by today's standards, they were a step forward in legitimizing lobbying. Even at a time in which the most commonly accepted norms of conduct were flagrantly abused, most lobbyists' functions were informational rather than seditious in nature, and the mere fact that their identities were to be revealed had a calming effect. Over the years, reasonable disclosure requirements have significantly reduced speculation about what lobbyists really do.

To this day, however, lobbyists uniformly object to fuller disclosure of their activities, but the objections are based primarily on the nuisance of complying with reams of government regulations rather than on a guilty conscience about untoward conduct. There is a fine line between reasonable disclosure and harassment that virtually forbids citizens to petition their own government for legitimate purposes. For example, under some of the proposals by so-called public interest groups in the mid-1970s, almost anyone who wrote to his or her congressman would have had to register as a lobbyist or be subject to civil and criminal sanctions. Other public interest groups, including Ralph Nader's Congress Watch, saw such proposals as an implicit threat to what they regarded as fundamental First Amendment guarantees.

Although most of the extreme proposals have since been defeated, the legal definition of lobbying remains one of the most controversial questions in the American political system, over which the Congress and the courts have labored on numerous occasions. However contentious the definition of lobbying may be, the laws that regulate the practice are very specific and must be observed.

Laws Regulating Lobbying

The original federal law regulating the activities of lobbyists dates to 1946 (60 *Stat.* 839 [August 2, 1946]). The Federal Regulation of Lobbying Act is basically a "sunshine law" that requires lobbyists to disclose what they do, on whose behalf they do it, and how much they are paid. Currently, lobbyists are required to report on a regular basis to the clerk of the House of Representatives. The information requested is merely a simple financial disclosure. Copies of the relevant regulations, the underlying legal provisions, and sample forms are avail-

---

*Washington professionals are as sensitive about referring to the legislative body as "*the* Congress" and not merely "Congress" as San Franciscans are about not referring to their city as "San Fran" or "Frisco."

able from the clerk's office. Since the law is constantly changing in this area, the lobbyist should be sure to check with the clerk regularly. Both the forms themselves and the instructions pertaining to them may be changed at any time.

Far more complex regulations apply if a lobbyist is working on behalf of foreign interests. The Foreign Agents Registration Act (52 *Stat.* 631 [June 8, 1938]) requires an explicit listing of all political activities undertaken by a lobbyist on behalf of any foreign principal. The definition of "foreign principal" includes both governmental and nongovernmental clients. Unless you are acting in a strictly legal capacity (exclusively as legal counsel to the foreign principal) you may be subject to this act. Failure to register and report on a semiannual basis to the Department of Justice can lead to severe criminal and civil sanctions. The Department of Justice regularly publishes booklets on the requirements of the Foreign Agents Registration Act. For more current information regarding the status of this act write to the Foreign Agents Registration Section, Criminal Division, United States Department of Justice, Washington, DC 20530.

Lobbying as a Vital Part of the American Political System

Despite infrequent revelations of abuse, lobbying remains one of the best protections our country has against extremism. Many other countries are familiar with "decree laws," which are adopted without consultation with competing groups, and which tend to foster radical rather than gradual change. But such laws are totally alien to the American political system. Our system has built-in delays that permit groups to form to support or oppose congressional legislation. A Newtonian law of politics might state that every political cause will ultimately engender an equal and opposite cause, and if these competing philosophies are allowed to meet—not just in the marketplace of ideas but in the reality of legislation—we will ultimately protect the system itself from zealotry.

The term "special interest group," like the word "lobbyist," has attracted a kind of reprobation that is altogether undeserved. While editorial writers and so-called reformers decry the very existence of special interests, nothing could be more traditionally American than the promotion of various ideas through combined effort. Every citizen is a special interest who must be considered in the process of shaping the law of the land. Blacks, consumers, teachers, pro-choicers, gun control advocates, handicapped people, aliens, exporters, and salesmen—all are special interests whose views deserve to be heard. There is not an

American today who is not represented (whether he or she knows it or not) by at least a dozen special interest groups.

Indeed, most of those who condemn the special interests are special interests themselves. John Gardner's Common Cause, the various Nader groups, and even the *Washington Post* have clearly defined vested interests for which they aggressively lobby. Some groups purport to represent the public interest in order to distinguish their objectives from the allegedly selfish goals of their opponents. Although such a label undoubtedly provides good copy for the media, and many public interest groups' members honestly believe they are promoting the common good, it is clear that all citizens do not share their values. One person's public interest is another's despotism; the mere label is not definitive. Is it more in the public interest to increase parkland at the expense of industrial development or to create jobs for minorities at the expense of the environment? These are public interest *questions*, but not public interest answers.

This is not to suggest that these self-styled public interest groups do not serve a valuable function, but merely that there is virtually no lobbying group—no matter how it chooses to label itself—that is not a special interest. Thus, the debate about the perceived evils of special interests is largely an exercise in polemics. Rather than decry the legitimacy of such groups, we should recognize them for what they are: the grass roots of the American political process. Citizen participation in government should be encouraged rather than condemned as some sleazy practice of the privileged. The purpose of this book is to enable more special interests to participate in the political process.

On a personal level, lobbyists can derive immense satisfaction from knowing that they have helped shape the political, social, and even moral foundation of this country. In short, lobbying is no more a dirty business than any other profession. Although it has its share of reprobates, so do the medical, legal, and stock-car-driving professions. This is not to excuse malfeasance among those who lobby; they have a special trust and the stakes are simply too high to permit license for those who would abuse it.

2

WHAT'S THE ISSUE?

"Politics, n. Strife of interests masquerading as a contest of principles."

—Ambrose Bierce

Single-Issue Lobbies

In the past twenty years, there has been a remarkable transformation in the American political system. Although party platforms have always had planks on issues ranging from national defense to farm policy, and special interest groups have traditionally played a role in the development of these planks, it is only in the last two decades that single-issue groups have had the enormous impact on public policy that they have today.*

Formerly, political parties and candidates attempted to balance the conflicting interests of the voters by supporting legislation that most of their constituents would like most of the time. While no one group would be completely satisfied with a given candidate or party, a carefully planned "consensus approach" virtually guaranteed moderation on most issues, whatever the candidate's partisan label. This, in turn, gave members of Congress the freedom to take controversial stands on particular issues, without fear of losing their seats because of one or two unpopular votes.

All this has changed. Special interest groups have learned that to be truly effective, they must be willing to base their support of a candidate on his or her stand on single issues, regardless of whether they agree with other aspects of the

---

*As with most phrases regarding lobbying, the "single-issue" designation is deceptive. No knowledgeable person would suggest that proponents of the Equal Rights Amendment were lobbying for a single issue; the implications of the women's rights movement go far beyond the mere adoption of a constitutional amendment. Even gun control advocates do not see themselves as part of a single-issue lobby; dozens of laws and social policies would be affected if they were successful in their campaign. "Single-issue," as used here, is meant only to distinguish groups that concentrate on one aspect of government policy from broad-based associations and trade unions, which consider dozens of unrelated legislative topics simultaneously.

candidate's platform. Whatever else a candidate may do, he or she must vote with these special interest groups on individual items or face the loss of their support. The special interest groups, on the other hand, do not have to weigh gains for their cause against other political considerations; in fact, they often have nothing else to consider. The trend toward stronger single-issue lobbies is particularly prevalent with regard to more emotional topics—environmental issues, abortion rights, gun control, and so forth.

While there is considerable debate about whether this trend bodes well for the traditional moderation of the American system, few informed commentators would deny that it has become a significant factor in electoral politics. In addition, the rise of the single-issue lobby has involved many more people in the legislative process.

Multiple-Issue Lobbies

Although single-issue special interest groups have proliferated over the past two decades, the most powerful lobbies in Washington are still multiple-issue lobbies such as labor unions, business organizations, and trade associations. These groups have traditionally tended to be flexible in their approach to politics. At any given time they may be working on a dozen different pieces of legislation that could affect their members in different ways. They are thus much more likely to accept compromise to achieve their overall goals. For example, a trade union may reluctantly back away from a hard stand on an environmental issue to gain votes on minimum wage legislation.

To do this successfully, the large multiple-issue lobbies must be highly sophisticated. Often, their lobbying activities are tightly controlled by a legislative director with years of experience in the art of compromise and political hardball. If multiple-issue lobbies do not have this kind of control, they tend to be crushed by their own diversity. They either fight every issue with equal ferocity or give up on the verge of victory, thus squandering their own power.

Size alone rarely determines a group's political effectiveness. The larger a group becomes, the more difficult it is to control. Some of the largest industrial trade associations in the country have dismal records of success in lobbying, whereas some smaller groups and unions have admirable batting averages.

Growth itself sometimes makes an association less powerful. As an association becomes more diverse, the likelihood that there will be internal conflict becomes greater. Such conflicts may be not only philosophical but also economic. For example, a union's trade workers may oppose imported products as threats to their jobs; but its retail clerks who sell both foreign and domestic goods may believe that imports keep prices down, thus increasing consumer spending and creating a greater need for *their* jobs.

The same dichotomies occur in industrial organizations, and even in so-called public interest groups, when they attempt to broaden their membership. A striking example of this has been the debate over wind farms. Some environmentalists tout wind-generated power as the ultimate renewable resource, while others decry building "industrial complexes" in areas where the vistas are just as plentiful as the wind.

Thus, although the multiple-issue lobbies are by far the largest and still the most powerful in Washington, their influence is not absolute. The rise of single- or restricted-issue organizations is testimony to the fact that the huge trade unions and business groups do not have a monopoly on the course of legislative affairs.

Identifying the Issue

Most novice lobbyists would find it presumptuous if someone suggested that they had not defined the issue they wanted to support or oppose. Yet one of the reasons most lobbying campaigns fail is that the lobbyists do not have a firm grasp of either the primary or ancillary issues involved in their campaign. Even the most apparently straightforward political issue may have legal and social repercussions that a novice would not foresee. The most laudable goals—for instance, the prevention of cancer—have been met with controversy because well-intentioned promoters did not fully understand the issues involved. They should have realized, for example, that a law banning any cancer-causing substance might ultimately wind up prohibiting all sorts of delicacies relished by the American public, and that such a law, if enforced, could damage the credibility of the lawmakers themselves.

There has never been a political goal desired by any group that did not have effects beyond the stated objective of its sponsors. There really is no such thing as a single-issue political goal. By the very nature of politics, there will always be a number of issues in play. This being the case, before lobbyists undertake any actual lobbying in the field, they must first do adequate homework.

3

HOMEWORK

"Laws are inherited like diseases."

—Johann Wolfgang von Goethe

Research on the Issue

No matter how clever your interest group's members are, inevitably someone has already thought of any ideas you may have. There is little satisfaction in reinventing the wheel, so your first obligation should be to spend a lot of time in the library. As noted in chapter 2, your research should consider not only the factual and philosophical justifications for your position, but also the effects its institutionalization would have on other issues.

For the purposes of this book, to avoid belittling any current ideologies, we will follow the planning and execution of a lobbying campaign launched by the Flat Earth Society, a mythical organization whose mission is to promote the planar nature of the planet and stamp out the heresy of Round Earthism. The scenario is as follows: The Flat Earth Society has chapters in twenty-six states and the District of Columbia, and twenty-seven hundred active members. Although it has been engaged in a number of legislative battles over the years, it is now facing its greatest challenge. A bill has been introduced in the House of Representatives that would not only ban the teaching of Flat Earth theory in public schools receiving federal money, but also provide federal funds to promote the concept that the planet is a sphere. This, of course, strikes at the very heart of Flat Earth theology, and the society is geared up to turn back the assault.

When the Flat Earth researchers begin to do their homework, they first undertake to uncover all related issues. The following is their preliminary list:

- The proposed legislation would increase government spending and thus spur inflation.

+Possible constitutional questions would be raised regarding the freedom of speech and religion.

+Federal bureaucracy would be increased to administer the program.

+The time spent on Round Earth instruction would take time away from teaching "basic" courses (mathematics, reading, etc.), to the detriment of minorities.

+Teachers might support Round Earthism as a way of increasing the number of jobs in their profession.

+Federal standards of instruction for primary schools would undermine the authority of local school boards to set curriculum. Thus, school boards might be allies of the Flat Earth Society.

+The defense establishment would probably argue that Round Earth theory is "advanced technology." They would likely contend that instruction in this "science" is necessary to maintain a military edge over rogue states and others who wish us harm.

+The mapmakers' position is unknown; they might support the Flat Earth cause as a ploy to require the creation of more new maps.

+Since Flat Earth maps are different from Round Earth maps, surveying changes could affect the boundaries of large properties (e.g., farms). The net political effect is unknown.

+International navigation rules would have to be altered to reflect whichever theory prevails, thus creating the possibility of foreign policy problems.

+This is another example of the federal government's intrusion into private lives—today Round Earth, tomorrow Big Brother.

Although many of the examples listed above may appear ludicrous to those of us with common sense, they are exactly the types of questions raised in actual lobbying campaigns. If your effort is heavily contested, you can be certain that apparently absurd (or at least imaginative) issues will be discussed during the course of the debate. It is best if you can be briefed on as many of them as possible *before* you announce your group's intentions. Members of Congress and congressional staffs have an uncanny knack for asking questions such as "How would your proposal affect the fishing catch in the Bering Sea?"—and giving you five ways it could. You had better know the answers before you are asked.

Know Your Enemies

One of the greatest mistakes you can make as a lobbyist is to assume that just because your opponents disagree with you, they must be a pack of scoundrels and idiots. Particularly on emotional issues, it is sometimes difficult to acknowledge that your opposition have a cumulative intelligence quotient of more than two digits. After all, if they were so smart, they would be able to see the merit of your views. Unfortunately, they probably feel the same way about you. Never underestimate their intelligence, fortitude, and commitment.

The best thing to do is to find out as much as possible about your opponents: who they are, who supports them, and what their arguments are. A good first step is to get your hands on as much of their propaganda as possible—pamphlets, books, newspaper articles, and Web pages. Your research committee should review anything in which they have made a public statement. This will give you a good initial idea of the types of arguments you can expect to face on the Hill. It may be that you have identified some issues that your opponents have not recognized, but you should first be sure you can persuasively rebut the arguments they believe are important.

Try to identify groups that have joined your opponents or could be expected to sympathize with the views they espouse. You should speculate about groups who may not have sided with your opponents but whose interests would seem to be best served by doing so. It is better to anticipate the worst than to be surprised later. At the same time, don't write off another group as an opponent until it has actually taken action against you. You don't want any more enemies than necessary, and it is sometimes possible to neutralize potential opponents through judicious compromise.

According to the mythology of lobbying, your next step would be to get involved in behind-the-scenes groping for personal "dirt" on the leadership of your opposition. This, however, is not only tasteless; it is amateurish, too. Aside from a few exceptional cases, such as President Clinton's extramarital escapades, personal peccadilloes do not have much effect on the Washington scene. Even raising issues such as your opponent's love life can be counterproductive; people on the Hill might be bemused by spicy revelations, but they will hardly respect you or your organization for publicizing them.

The exception to this rule is when you can conclusively demonstrate that your opponents have either lied or substantially misrepresented their true objectives. For example, if you came across credible evidence that an environmental group was secretly funded by polluting industries, under certain circumstances you might be wise to reveal it. But be careful—if you come across information of this nature, don't get "buck fever." Settle down, check your facts again, check your own closet for skeletons, and take very, very careful aim before squeezing the trigger. Your own credibility is at stake as much as your opponents'. If you make unsubstantiated claims about them, you will suffer more than they.

One final note: it is almost always a bad idea to pull a stunt like planting an informant in your opponent's camp. If the informant is discovered and you are exposed, your credibility will plummet and your entire campaign may be lost (remember Watergate), and it is highly unlikely you would discover anything from infiltration that you could not gain through diligent scholarship. With the stakes as high as they are, it makes little sense to risk your entire program for a juvenile attempt at espionage.

This is not to say your opponents won't be tempted to try spying. The best protection you have from this possibility is not stiff security measures, but your own integrity. The only useful information your opponents could discover by infiltrating your operation would be on some off-the-wall stunt you yourself may be planning. Fight hard and fight clean. That's not moralizing; it's practical. If you have both credibility and the facts, you have the battle half won.

Know Your Friends

Most successful lobbying campaigns spend more time and energy cultivating friends than denouncing enemies. Like identification of the issues, identification of friends is extremely important. If there are any groups that could be affected positively by your plans (there will be dozens), contact them. You can broaden your influence far beyond the membership of your group if you can legitimately claim the endorsement of other organizations. Better yet, these groups can lend you money, manpower, and expertise that might otherwise be unavailable to you. In most cases the more diverse your alliance, the better. An unbeatable combination would be an ad hoc alliance of the AFL-CIO, U.S. Chamber of Commerce, AARP, NRA, Sierra Club, and American Israel Public Affairs Committee. Unlikely though it seems, stranger coalitions have been formed.

In your search for friends, you should base your decisions on the issues presented, not the general philosophical inclination of your potential allies. Some of the most successful lobbying groups have been composed of such traditionally antagonistic forces as labor and management (international trade law); conservative Westerners and environmentalists (conservation issues); religious cults and the Eastern press (First Amendment questions); and Communists and energy companies (nuclear power). Don't let initial distaste dissuade you from forming temporary alliances with otherwise unsympathetic groups. This is hardball politics, not a college debating society, and the credibility of your campaign can be enhanced by bringing together apparently disparate groups. Swallow your prejudices and do it.

This advice may seem somewhat counterintuitive, since politics is often portrayed as a vicious battle between the forces of darkness and light. In fact, politics is the art of compromise. You will generally find that accommodation is a much better tactic than absolutism—especially if it gets you allies. Partial victories are much better than defeat, and you will be able to build on the progress you have made.

When courting potential friends, the first thing you should recognize is that they rarely volunteer. Organizations whose members are politically experienced will not join you for purely philosophical reasons; you will have to show them very specific ways your issue will benefit them. You will also have to remind your allies of promises they have made regarding their support. Undying oaths of friendship carry little practical weight; you will have to spend as much time giving backbone transfusions to your allies as you do in the political trenches on Capitol Hill.

To the uninitiated this can be a frustrating and disillusioning experience. Promises will be broken, personal vendettas begun, and outright treason committed; but you are still best served by having allies. It's hard to live with them, but you can't live without them. Toughen your hide and sharpen your tongue. "Keep your troops in line" is the most important and most frequently disregarded axiom of lobbying.

On the other hand, your group will probably also be approached by others seeking *your* help. Rules to follow in such a situation:

+Make sure it is in your group's interest to support the proposal itself. Never agree to an alliance merely because you believe the group making the request could be valuable to you at some future date. Lobbyists tend to have very short memories.

+Never make promises you cannot or do not intend to keep. You should be very specific about what you will and will not do and vague about areas you wish to consider further before committing to. Never leave the other group with the impression you promised something that you didn't. Your credibility is as important with your allies as it is with members of Congress.

The ground rules of these fragile alliances should be very clearly set out. Don't attempt to bait your ally on issues unrelated to the problem at hand. All that will breed is suspicion and dissension. Don't expect to turn around your newfound friends on every matter, but be sure you don't compromise on any issue unrelated to the current project.

What's the Law?

You may conceive of your group as more concerned about policy than legal technicalities, but if you are involved in lobbying, your ultimate objective is to change the provisions of existing statutes. It is not enough to say that you want to support clean water or even to clean up Walnut Creek. Your group's real objective is to amend Section 14(b)(2)(ii). You must know not only the general objectives of your project, but also how the new law should actually read. This is not just a lobbying tactic. Clever lawyers representing your opponents will probably take the new law to court. If you have made any errors, or if the law's intent is unclear, they will tie the statute in knots for years to come.

If you are not a lawyer, the best way to determine the status of the current law and the way you would like to revise it is to request a "legal memorandum" (*not* an opinion letter) from an experienced law firm. This request should be made very early in any lobbying campaign. There is no substitute for a carefully researched analysis of the way current law has been interpreted by the courts and a cross-check of other laws that would be affected if your position were implemented. To paraphrase Congressman Michael Myers, convicted of bribery in the Abscam investigation, "Specifics talk and bullshit walks."

Although this process may appear to merely create work for lawyers, it is ultimately a bargain. If you fail to get sound legal advice at the outset, you are almost guaranteed to pay ridiculous fees to correct the problems that will arise later. But be sure to agree *in advance* on the approximate cost of such a project; law firms make a great deal of money from open-ended assignments.

Who Are the Players?

Once you have recognized enemies, recruited friends, and determined the status of the law, you need to locate the individuals on the Hill who will consider your issue. These are your "target members." They will be your primary focus in your lobbying campaign.

When legislation is introduced in either the House or the Senate, it is immediately referred to a committee. (Do not be misled by the names of the committees. For example, extensive jurisdiction over international trade matters rests with the Senate Finance Committee—not the Foreign Relations Committee.) Although the committee structure is rather complex (see chapter 8), you should be able to determine which of its subcommittees will consider your bill; check with the staff of the full committee if you are unsure. Once you know the appropriate committee and subcommittee, you can start making your list of congressional contacts.

First, list all appropriate committee and subcommittee members (by party) and all the members of the House Rules Committee (the Rules Committee considers almost all legislation at one point or another). You can get these names via THOMAS (http://thomas.loc.gov), publications such as the *Congressional Directory* or *Congressional Yellow Book*, or directories published by special interest groups. Next, list the names of all congressmen and senators traditionally on your side of the issue. You can get a general idea of their voting patterns by reviewing *The Almanac of American Politics* and seeing which ones have voted on similar issues in the past. This information is also available in greater detail from the House and Senate study committees, which have computerized analyses of all "record votes." (See chapter 19 for more information on all these sources.)

Finally, you should categorize every member on your list according to your access to him or her. For instance, is anyone in your organization a constituent of the member's state or district? Does anyone have a personal connection to the member or someone on the member's staff? Would the legislation have an immediate effect on the member's state or district? List every access route to each member on your list, then determine how best to approach him or her, through either your own members or the allies you have cultivated.

At this stage it is also important to identify the administrative agency—for instance, the Department of Education, or the Department of Agriculture—that will have primary responsibility for enforcing the legislation with which you are concerned. Without its support, the executive branch will likely oppose you actively on the Hill, and the administration can field more lobbyists than you can. It is essential that you at least neutralize their opposition.

The government has grown so complex that it is a virtual certainty that more than one agency would be affected by any piece of legislation. For example, an environmental bill may have an impact upon programs of the Department of Defense (strategic materials, military reservations, defense contractors, etc.), the Department of Labor (lost jobs), and the Department of Energy (development of new energy sources). Therefore, you should look not only to the primary administrative agency but also to the other departments and bureaus that would be touched by your project. The legal memorandum mentioned earlier should help you identify all the possibilities. You should ask your attorneys to include them as part of their assignment.

Even if the primary agency is opposed to your position, don't give up hope. Contrary to popular opinion, the government is not a monolith, and agencies are as jealous of their own interests as private lobbying groups are of theirs. Some other agency is almost certain to support you due to its institutional hatred of the primary agency. Allies within the administration can be a valuable source of information on interagency bickering; be sure to list all competing agencies you uncover in your initial chart of "friends," and approach them early in the lobbying campaign.

The support of another agency does not necessarily mean the executive branch will back your position, but open disagreement among the various executive departments can effectively hamstring organized opposition to your point of view. If you think the agency that would ordinarily be charged with administering your program would be hostile to your position, it may be wise to sow the seeds of dissent among competing agencies.

Competing agencies can also give you an unsurpassed advantage if you convince them to issue reports supporting your position, even if the ultimate decision of the administration is to oppose you. Most agencies have the legal authority to publish studies, "white papers," etc. that may not conform to the administration line. Since these reports are given great credence on the Hill, and they have often been used successfully to undercut the "official" administration position, any time you spend with administrative agencies is well invested.

The Resource Book

Once you have completed your homework, it must be organized into a usable format. This resource book will be your bible throughout the lobbying campaign. It is best to set it up in a three-ring, loose-leaf notebook so changes can be easily made. A sample format is as follows:

+ **Existing Law:** Photocopies of existing federal statutes, tab-indexed; pertinent sections highlighted or underlined.

+ **Legal Memoranda:** Legal memoranda prepared by your attorneys as described in this chapter.

+ **Opponents:** Addresses, telephone numbers, e-mail addresses, and leadership names; photocopied samples of propaganda they have distributed regarding your subject.

+ **Allies:** Addresses, telephone numbers and, e-mail addresses; narrative descriptions of the subissues about which your allies are particularly concerned. It is important to include the names of as many contact persons, both in Washington and in the field, as possible.

+**Congressional Contacts:** Information on all members of Congress who will have direct contact with your measure on a committee level, as well as all known congressional allies and opponents. Each entry should each be separately tab-indexed, and should include the member's name, office address, telephone numbers, e-mail addresses, complete staff, congressional district map (for congressmen), and biography, and a list of constituents of the member's state or district with whom you have direct contact.

+**Administrative Agencies:** Information on all administrative agencies that would be affected by your proposal, including a narrative description of each one's position on your issue. You should list names, addresses, telephone numbers, and e-mail addresses of all contacts in the agency so you can communicate with them rapidly.

+**Issues:** A list of various issues that could be raised during the course of the debate on your proposed legislation. The issues, and your views on them, should be stated succinctly. This section is the most important of the entire resource book and is the "party line" you will expect your members to follow when questioned. It must be very carefully edited and proofread, and should incorporate every issue you can conceive of. This section should be heavily footnoted with the sources of your information and should include charts, statistics, etc. upon which your argument relies. Remember, this is *your group's* resource book, and it will not be given to individual congressional offices. Do not attempt to abridge any of the data here.

The resource book is a very sensitive document and should not be widely distributed, even among members of your own group. You should institute several controls to limit distribution, including marking each copy with a "control number." These control numbers should be assigned to specific people within your organization, who should then be charged with maintaining confidentiality. Carelessness and incompetence are more common than treachery in Washington, but Judases abound as well, so you need to be very careful about who gets access to the family jewels. With the exception of the "Issues" section, the resource book should *not* be taken to the Hill during your contacts with congressional offices. The "Issues" section should be taken on Hill visits so you can refer to it in meetings with members and staff. This will help you to immediately—and consistently—respond to any questions or objections to your position. However, you must maintain control even over this portion of the resource book. *Do not* lose it or give it to anyone outside your group.

Although putting together a resource book may seem rather painstaking work, the time spent in carefully researching your issue and making sure your supporters understand it is worthwhile. If you have done your job properly, you will not have to do additional research on questions that arise during the course of a campaign; you will have considered them already. In short, the resource book is the document most valuable to a lobbyist's campaign.

4

THE ACTION PLAN

"General Good is the plea of the scoundrel, hypocrite, and flatterer."

—William Blake

You have finished your research and identified your issues, your friends, and your enemies, but it is still not time to attack the Hill. First you must develop a thorough plan for implementing the research you have already done. This "action plan" is more than a calendar of campaign events; it is your line of battle, and it includes schedules, names of the players, and the methods by which you will implement your entire campaign.

The best action plans are the product of several people's thinking, so share your ideas with others in your group. It is generally best, however, not to attempt to write an action plan in a committee meeting but rather to circulate drafts among your members and work out details together later. The final action plan will be a highly confidential document, and it should be distributed only to those in your group directly involved with the actual lobbying.

Like the resource book, the action plan should be arranged in a three-ring, loose-leaf binder for ease of revision. The precise content of each section will be dealt with in subsequent chapters, but a general breakdown is below.

Press Relations

How members of the press perceive your lobbying campaign is crucial, especially if your position is controversial. Therefore, be particularly sensitive to the issues described in chapter 5. The action plan regarding press relations should include the following:

Press Contacts

Since the media constitute one of your most important means of communicating your views to the public, this section of your action plan should specify all persons who are authorized to speak for your group to the press. Explicitly list the names of one or two authorized press contacts; all others should refer inquiries to them.

Although this may appear to be an undemocratic or oppressive policy, it is a necessary precaution. Many organizations have more press spokespeople than they have members, a fact that the media is fond of exploiting to imply internal dissension. The worst thing you can do is to permit just anyone to represent your group's views to the public.

The press contacts section should also include the names, addresses, telephone numbers, and e-mail addresses of reporters for publications that have an interest in your issue. *Hudson's Washington News Media Contacts Directory*, listed in chapter 19, provides this information. Your press contacts list should not include every reporter or publication listed in *Hudson's*, only those with whom you have a reasonable working relationship. If you would like to include others, be sure to indicate those individuals with whom you have personal contact with an asterisk or some other symbol. All the reporters on your press contacts list should receive copies of your organization's press releases as they become available.

Clearance Procedures

Few issues can lead to more acrimony within a group than unauthorized press releases, so this section should describe in detail the procedures you intend to follow when issuing official statements to the media. It is generally best if only one person be designated to prepare press statements. These draft statements, however, should always be reviewed by several other high-ranking persons in your group. Outline the procedures for how such clearances should be accomplished. The clearance methodology should be agreed on in advance by as many people as possible, but the procedure itself should be rather simple. Three—at most four—individuals should be given sole discretion to decide on the release's final form. Most news items are time sensitive, so you should not wait for a formal meeting, but instead establish a protocol for approving the releases over the telephone or by e-mail.

This section should also specify the contact persons who can answer additional questions about your press releases, and make it clear that their names should be included in every release. These people should be the same individuals authorized to clear the original press release. Within your group you should discuss the nature and extent of additional information these contact persons are authorized to disclose. Although you cannot anticipate every question the press might ask in a particular case (they are geniuses at formulating embarrassing queries), your action plan should set down some general guidelines. To be sure that all answers to press inquiries will be consistent, your spokesperson should parrot the information contained in the resource book.

Aside from providing general information about your group's membership, you should rarely respond to questions regarding the internal politics of your organization. Press speculation about internal differences of opinion makes good copy for them, but it also guarantees dissension within your ranks. The rule when answering such questions is to refuse to speculate. If absolutely necessary, you can put the best slant on any problems you have, noting (with as straight a face as you can manage) that "the diversity of views in our group is our strength."

Congressional Contacts

This is one of the most complex sections of your action plan, and as such, it should be extensively annotated and cross-indexed. Much of the information in this section should already have been prepared for your resource book, but it should be edited according to the specific needs of the action plan. For example, some of the congressional contacts in your resource book may not be targeted in your lobbying efforts, in which case they need not be listed here.

The format of this section can vary according to the needs of your group but should include at least the following:

+Names, addresses, telephone numbers, and e-mail addresses of key members of Congress, particularly those assigned to committees that will be considering your issue.

+Names, addresses, telephone numbers, and e-mail addresses of members of Congress with whom your group has exceptionally good relations, particularly in those states or districts where your organization is strong, whether or not those members sit on the committees directly affected by your issue.

+Contacts on the staffs of both committees and members of Congress. This section is extremely important (see chapter 11). The staff list should include each staff member's personal telephone numbers and e-mail addresses, and describe any previous contact you may have had with him or her. It should also include any further relevant details about the staff member's background.

✦Congressional demographics. You should prepare a complete demographic sketch of the congressional district or state represented by each member of Congress whom you list. Include a district map where appropriate and an analysis of the district (see *The Almanac of American Politics*, described in chapter 19). You should also include an analysis of any constituent relationships that members of your group may have with the member of Congress.

✦Complete analysis of each member of Congress listed and that member's voting record on similar issues. These are available from the various Senate and House study committees (see details in chapter 19).

✦Incidental information about ancillary groups' influence with individual members of Congress and the method by which the members may be approached through such groups.

Letters

Your action plan should contain a section devoted to your letter-writing campaign, which should be conducted according to the guidelines in chapter 6. This section of the plan should contain a sample format for letters to the Hill and a check-off list to track the letters sent. The list should include all the congressional contacts listed above, cross-referenced by the members of your group with whom they have constituent relationships. Organizing the list can become a bit complex, particularly since each of your members necessarily has a constituent relationship with several members of Congress. One way to simplify things is to prepare spreadsheets using Excel or, better yet, Access, which can sort each member of Congress and each of your members into separate fields, together with a check-off field to indicate when letters were sent, by whom, and to whom.

E-mail attachments (preferable) or photocopies of all letters sent to the Hill should be forwarded to your group's headquarters or to a committee established for this purpose. That committee will be responsible for assuring compliance with the letter-writing assignments. This committee should also be responsible for preparing response letters to members of Congress who request further information, or whose replies contain errors that need to be corrected. The constituent who sent the original letter should sign such follow-ups; the drafting committee should not respond to the member on its own initiative.

All this might seem a rather elaborate system for putting a few words down on paper, but more lobbying campaigns have been ruined by friends than by enemies. As some contemporary politicians have shown us, it is quite easy to shoot yourself in the foot in Washington; the best way to avoid this fate is to keep the safety on, even when it involves a little more effort.

Demonstrations

As you will see in chapter 7, demonstrations are rarely as effective as a well-planned lobbying campaign. Get your members off the streets and into the halls of the Congress, where they can make a much greater impact. Demonstrations are sometimes the only alternative, however, when you have a large, loosely structured "cause" and it is impossible to effectively direct the activities of your membership. If, for whatever reason, you decide that a demonstration is necessary or desirable, it should be very carefully planned.

The demonstrations section of your action plan should include at least the following:

+ Date, time, and place of the demonstration.

+ Names, addresses, telephone numbers, and e-mail addresses of groups expected to participate in the demonstration, together with names of the leaders of such groups.

+ Names, addresses, telephone numbers, and e-mail addresses of all public authorities (including the police) with whom you have spoken while arranging for permits and other logistics. (You should keep photocopies of any permits you receive.)

+ List of speakers invited to the demonstration, time and place of their appearances, and subject matter of their remarks.

+ Logistical details: names and addresses of companies or organizations supplying materials (e.g., sound equipment, bullhorns, posters) for your demonstration. This section should also detail who made the original contacts, what the cost of the materials will be, and who will be responsible for delivering them or picking them up. Any agreements made with suppliers should be very specific. If, for example, the sound equipment does not arrive at the right place at the right time, or it does not work as anticipated, your demonstration could be ruined.

+ Housing information. If you are expecting a large demonstration, including many people of moderate means, housing must be arranged well in advance. This section of your action plan should list all places where demonstrators can be bivouacked before and after the rally (e.g., churches that are willing to provide temporary housing).

+ Plans for providing marshals. It is always best if your group can provide its own security. The action plan should establish programs to recruit and train as many marshals as it will take to keep your demonstration from being marred by outside police action.

+ Transportation arrangements. Parking for private cars in Washington is difficult to find and outrageously expensive. The traditional way to transport demonstrators from outside the Washington area to the rally is by bus. Buses should be chartered by your local groups (not by the central coordinating branch), but the action plan should have a complete list of all buses, their estimated time of arrival, and parking arrangements.

+ Instructions. The action plan should include a one- or two-page instruction sheet that will be provided to all demonstrators. It will include such information as parade route and time, rally location and speakers, housing location and cost, instructions on obeying marshals, and procedures for demonstrators to follow if they are arrested. The instructions should also include the one-page fact sheet on your issue that will be described in chapter 6.

+ Procedures for dealing with arrests and detentions. Even in the best-planned and most well-intentioned demonstration, some overzealous participant is likely to be arrested. The more emotional the issue, the more likely it is that arrests will occur. This section of your action plan should outline procedures for your organization to follow in the event that any members of your group are detained by the police. It should include names, addresses, telephone numbers, and e-mail addresses of public defenders (and other lawyers); names, addresses, telephone numbers, and e-mail addresses of responsible police officials; name, address, phone number, and e-mail address of the prosecuting attorney's office; and names, addresses, telephone numbers, and e-mail addresses of the individuals in your group assigned to coordinate the release of your arrested members.

The above list is not comprehensive. The logistics of even a moderate-sized demonstration are truly astonishing. Subcommittees should be convened for each of the issues listed above and a responsible individual designated to oversee each of the functions. Your demonstration coordinating committee, composed of all subcommittee chairmen, should meet frequently prior to the demonstration. If any one of the items listed above is not carefully planned in advance, your demonstration may be not only ineffectual, but also downright disastrous.

Gimmicks

Gimmicks (discussed more fully in chapter 14) are primarily designed to attract media attention. They can take almost any form; their variety is limited only by your ingenuity. If you intend to use such devices in your lobbying campaign, the action plan should contain the following:

+ description of the gimmicks to be employed
+ persons within your group responsible for planning and coordinating the gimmicks, plus names, addresses, telephone numbers, and e-mail addresses of vendors as appropriate
+ permits or other licenses necessary to pull off the gimmick
+ media representatives whom you will contact for coverage of your gimmick
+ all other logistical details relating to the legality and the practicality of your gimmick

As with demonstrations, most successful gimmicks are much more complicated to put into practice than they first appear. Careful planning is essential if they are to be effective.

The Hill Blitz

The "Hill blitz" is a traditional yet very effective method of direct lobbying. It has the advantage of involving your members in face-to-face meetings with members of Congress and Hill staff. If you have the members and the time, a Hill blitz is always more effective than a demonstration or gimmick.

The Hill blitz section of the action plan, although rudimentary, is one of the most difficult to prepare. A well-structured Hill blitz will require hundreds of telephone calls and careful supervision. Full details on how to put one together are contained in chapter 15, but for now just be sure that your action plan includes the following:

+ Names, telephone numbers, local (Washington) addresses, and e-mail addresses of all participants in the blitz.
+ Names, titles, addresses, telephone numbers, and e-mail addresses of all persons to be contacted on the Hill. The list should include each member of

Congress of whom a blitz participant is a constituent, members who have given you the most support, chairmen of committees and subcommittees involved with your issue, and all other members who may have a direct impact on your cause. In most cases, your list will probably not exceed forty-five members of Congress.

+Complete cross-index of dates, times of appointments, and individuals to be involved. The list of all appointments relevant to your individual members should be given to each one. Other logistical details, including the dates and times of luncheons, parties, dinners, receptions, and breakfasts, should be included in the master list.

The appointments cross-index is the heart of the Hill blitz plan, and you should allocate ample time for its preparation. Although it appears rather simple, development of a comprehensive appointments list can be extremely time-consuming and frustrating.

Other

Depending on the nature of your campaign, you may have a number of other sections in your action plan. They could include the following:

+calendars of events: dates of congressional hearings, etc.

+fundraising

+expenditures and political contributions (see chapter 13)

+resources: contingency plans for your group and "emergency" telephone numbers, names, addresses, and e-mail addresses

If the resource book is the heart of your lobbying campaign, the action plan is the guts. The more time you spend planning, the more likely you are to succeed. Even if you ultimately decide to retain a professional lobbyist, insist that he or she provide you with a detailed action plan. Vague promises simply do not cut ice in Washington.

5

THE PRESS

"All politics are based on the indifference of the majority."

—James Reston

In an ideal world, perhaps laws would be made by enlightened lawgivers who deliberated the merits of issues in unbiased forums, sequestered like jurors in a murder trial from the vagaries of the media. In the real world, lawmakers are subjected to a barrage of outside influences, the most powerful of which is the press.

Although some political theorists push the "insulation" option, it simply wouldn't work in the American political system, to which the influence of the press has always been fundamental. The authors of the Constitution institutionalized the press's role—virtually nowhere else in the world are journalists given the freedom and the responsibility to act as guardians against government excesses.

Contrary to the self-serving assertions of some journalism school professors, the media not only report the news, but also make the news. The mere appearance of a story in a major metropolitan daily can affect public opinion overnight. Media hype can make or break candidates for public office; although Richard Nixon was undeniably paranoid about the press, the Watergate scandal probably would not have resulted in his resignation if the *Washington Post* had not made such searing disclosures about his administration's antics.

You don't have to be Nixon to hate the press or Rupert Murdoch to love it, but as a lobbyist you must understand how it works.

Advertising

Anyone who has not been cloistered in a monastery for the past forty years realizes that advertising is one of today's most powerful forces. It can induce otherwise rational people to clandestinely squeeze toilet paper in supermarkets, forsake knives for plastic contraptions that squish tomatoes, and elect proven scoundrels to high public office. As powerful as this medium is, it should be accorded the same treatment as low-yield nuclear weaponry: it is expensive and devastatingly effective when used properly, but can be either a dud or downright dangerous to the user if handled carelessly.

One of the two most common mistakes political advertisers make is to believe they are competent to write their own copy. It may seem that any damn fool could write better ads than those portraying housewives reduced to tears over waxy yellow buildup, but in truth, advertising is a highly sophisticated art. There would be plenty of room for amateurs if ad space were not so expensive, but if your group is like most, you cannot afford to waste your money on slap-dash advertisements. Full-page *Washington Post* ads do the egos of the groups placing them a lot of good, but most are so poorly written that they do not convince anybody of anything. At seventeen thousand dollars or more per appearance, that is pretty expensive ego gratification. If you have a substantial advertising budget, you are best advised to seek professional help from an advertising agency.

One precautionary note: advertising executives are paid to produce effective ads, not to write erudite copy. Many groups have been dissatisfied with professional ad execs because they felt that the advertisements submitted were either juvenile or truncated. To an advertising person, simplicity is beautiful. You can always spot the ads in the *Washington Post* and the *New York Times* for which no advertising agency was consulted—foreign governments, in particular, have a penchant for publishing long diatribes by their glorious leaders—and these lengthy treatises are not read by anyone but academicians. If you pay for advertising advice, take it. You are not paying for a closely reasoned tome on the minutiae of your position; you are paying for results. You should not attempt to second-guess the professional advice you receive unless the ads submitted are grossly deceptive or scandalously mindless.

The other common mistake political advertisers make is to believe all (or any) of the advertising media's self-advertisement. Television, radio, magazines, and newspapers feverishly compete with one another to gain advertising revenues by making extravagant claims about their effectiveness. There are as many theories about effective advertising *means* as there are advertising *media*. For most groups, however, their limited treasuries can best be devoted to aspects of the media other than advertising. If your position has political value, it also has media value. You can achieve more by having your position carried in news stories than through paid advertisements.

How to Become Newsworthy

The first thing to understand about the editors of news outlets is that they tend to be conservative; that is, they would rather stick with issues that they know have a sustained, proven reader interest than to publish stories on new subjects with which they are unfamiliar. If your group or issue is relatively unknown, it is best to link your position with that of a more currently popular crusade. For example, the Flat Earth Society mentioned in chapter 3 could link its opposition to Round Earth teaching in public schools to a wide variety of more traditional causes such as inflation, big government, bureaucratic waste, or parents' rights.

A corollary to the general rule that familiarity breeds ink is that what is familiar to one editor may be Sanskrit to another. There are thousands of publications in the United States catering to virtually every conceivable interest. Your approach to editors and publishers should be multifaceted; do not gear your entire campaign toward what you think will appeal to the editor of the *Washington Post*. Editors of local newspapers like a more parochial slant on the issues; special interest publications need to know how your position would affect their readers. The basic rule in becoming newsworthy is to put yourself in the position of a viewer, listener, or reader of the news outlet you would like to carry your story. Editors respond to their customers' needs; their job is to sell papers.

Once you determine the proclivities of a particular publication, you should not wait to be "discovered" by them. Using your resource book (see chapter 3), call and visit the news outlets you have targeted. Almost all daily newspapers, radio stations, and even television broadcasters rely on wire services or networks as sources for their news, and they will generally be delighted to have an exclusive lead on a story of interest to their audiences. Reporters tend to be overworked and harassed, so the more written information you can provide to them the better off you will be. Don't be afraid to request a meeting with a contact's editor—behind the city desk you will find some hard-bitten types with their sleeves rolled up, but keep in mind that news outlets are businesses, and a reporter's bread and butter are the sources that will give him or her hard stories with which to impress the boss. Prepare your facts and ask for an opportunity to speak with the "powers that be."

As in all aspects of lobbying, your relations with the press must be characterized by complete candor. You are playing in the big leagues, so don't attempt to be cute with your facts; it will not work. You may get one story with inaccurate information, but if reporters and editors believe you have intentionally misled them, a dozen adverse stories will follow. Worse yet, stories on your side of the issue will never grace their pages or airwaves again.

To remain newsworthy over an extended period, you must retain the contacts you originally established and keep the press advised of the progress of your issue. You need not do anything particularly dramatic in this respect; merely keep your contacts in the loop. If you have established a rapport with some members of the press, it's a good idea to suggest follow-up stories.

Talking to Reporters: Good Guys and Bad Guys

Disabuse yourself of any image you have of the infallibility of reporters or their constant dedication to the truth. Reporters are paid to write stories for news outlets, news outlets exist to make money, and news stories must be turned out at a feverish pace that does not always leave time for background checks on the accuracy of items published or broadcast. Consequently, whether your media coverage is fair and accurate will depend on who is doing the reporting.

There is no law or journalistic canon that requires you to treat all reporters or all news outlets equally, and you do not have to roll over and play dead for every one of them that takes an interest in your cause. Publications do not have a constitutional right to probe your innermost thoughts on your issue; you have no obligation whatsoever to grant exclusive interviews to publications that consistently attack you. Nikita Khrushchev once said "We will bury the West with shovels they sell us." You are not required—even by the street-fighting rules of Washington politics—to provide ammunition for the bad guys.

You must be careful, however, not to define "bad guys" too broadly. A reporter's job is to report the news in an objective manner and to deal with you honestly. A "good guy" may not necessarily agree with your position or consistently write sympathetic articles on your behalf. It is not only unreasonable but downright foolish to expect a reporter to write favorable stories about your group merely because he or she has occasionally been given exclusive interviews.

Before you make decisions with regard to "good guys" and "bad guys," consider the following:

+ Have you received "good press" (as defined later in this chapter) from the publication concerned?
+ Has the journalist or editor always told you the truth (e.g., kept your name confidential when requested and never under those circumstances published a story in such a way that your identity was made public)?

If the answer to either of these questions is "no," then place that publication or reporter on your "gray list" (in politics no one is blacklisted—you never know when either they or you may be rehabilitated). The gray-listing of reporters or publications does not mean you will not speak to them under any circumstances, merely that they will not be favored with exclusive interviews, tips, or any off-the-record conversation. And if the "stick" you use against hostile press is exclusion from the inner circle, then your reward for the good guys is an understanding and sympathetic relationship.

The distinction between good guys and bad guys is manifest, but it cannot be pressed too far. Do not attempt to exclude "hostiles" from press conferences, media events, etc., or otherwise declare war on any news outlet. Remember, the free press belongs to the person who owns one. Unless you have majority stock ownership in a newspaper chain, do not try to beat the media at their own game. On the other hand, don't drop your guard because you think of a reporter as a good guy; if you speculate about the weaknesses in your particular issue, the reporter may feel duty-bound to report your musings, and the resulting report may give your opponents ideas that would not otherwise have occurred to them.

In short, don't be afraid to discriminate among representatives of the media, but don't start holy wars or give away the family store to your opposition.

What Is "Good Press"?

Good press certainly means more than having your name spelled right on the op-ed page. It does not mean, however, that a story that points out one or two of your warts is calamitous. Many so-called bad news stories, at which ordinary people would cringe, actually benefit the organization profiled. Being cast as the underdog can be an advantage in certain situations, and controversy is not necessarily bad; Ralph Nader has gained much of his strength by remaining controversial. It is only when the stories start to focus on subjects other than the issues you are promoting that you need to really worry.

Thus, it is easier to describe what good press is not than what it is. You should greet a media representation of your position with restrained joy if it *does not* fall into any of the following categories:

+ no press at all (your group is not mentioned; your issue is not mentioned; you are ignored)

+ "filler" stories about fringe groups (if you're put in the same category as the Put Pants on Dogs Movement or the Equal Rights for Avocados League, you're subject to such ridicule that your group may as well despair of gaining credibility with the press)

+ substantiated allegations that your group is merely a stalking horse for other interests whose identity is secret and perhaps in conflict with your stated goals

+accusations that your group's stated objective is not really your primary objective, but merely a subterfuge to accomplish other political or economic goals

+characterizations of your group as a bunch of fanatics or as closely allied with an extremist organization

+accusations of illegal or immoral activities, including association with known criminals (particularly mobsters or terrorist-funding groups)

+substantiated allegations that your group has consciously misrepresented facts to the press and the public or has attempted to cover up unethical or immoral activity

+allegations that your group has illegally or improperly benefited from personal contact with government officials responsible for the administration of programs you advocate

+stories concerning internal dissension within your group, particularly if such stories include references to improper conduct on the part of the leadership (e.g., embezzlement of money, unethical hiring practices, or internal directives to lie)

Whether and When to Say What—and to Whom

Decisions regarding statements to the press fall into two categories: when the press calls you and when you call them. The former situation is relatively easy to resolve. If reporters call, you should almost always speak to them, unless the caller is an absolutely unreformed bad guy. Such individuals should never be given exclusive interviews, even just over the phone. Deal with these people only at press conferences. If a friendly or neutral reporter calls, talk to that person. Even if you don't have a story, you will have demonstrated your accessibility.

It is more likely you will suffer from a common Washington malady: lack of press attention. In this case you will be driven to contacting the media rather than waiting for them to call you. Follow a few simple rules:

+Be credible. Be sure of your facts and never mislead a reporter.

+Don't call reporters until you have a real story. A generalized rendition of your position will not be of much interest to anyone unless you have a news "peg." Perhaps the most salient feature of a peg is immediacy. Don't call with information about something that took place months ago; a reporter is generally interested in events that either have just happened or are about to happen. Of course, most stories have historical antecedents that are important to the context of current events, but unless you can convey newly revealed evidence about an "old" story, stick with the "immediacy" rule.

◆Do not give "exclusive" interviews to too many people. If you put out an exclusive story with which everyone is already familiar, it is not very likely you will get the play you want in important publications. Worse, you will lose credibility.

◆Do not insist upon attribution of the story to your group. Reporters like to feel that they are independent and that they should be the sole judge of whether you or your group is mentioned. Your chances of being named are much greater if you do not insist upon it.

◆Be sure to warn any friendly reporters you call of potential land mines in a story and which facts they might want to cross-check, and to provide other sources and names of your opponents so they can get their views. One trick is to give the reporter the name of one of your leading opponents—someone you know to be hostile to the press. You have done your duty; you have warned the reporter about the existence of opposing views and provided access to those views. If your opponent wants to put a gun to his or her own head, that is your opponent's business. When giving the recommendation, be as disarming as possible. Don't attempt to state your opponent's case; merely say you don't understand the entire position but that the reporter should call so-and-so before writing the story to get an opposing opinion.

In any conversation with the press, it is important for you to firmly establish ground rules with the reporter unless you simply don't care what he or she writes (or attributes). "Off the record" to one reporter may mean something else to another, and there are subtle distinctions between "background," "deep background," "not for attribution," and "off the record." Be sure that both you and the reporter clearly understand the rules in advance of the interview. Of course, a reporter may refuse to accept your conditions. In that case, anything you say is fair game, and you should be very cautious with the sounds that come between your teeth. They will be thrown back at your molars very quickly if you make a mistake.

You should be very concerned when a story is published—even an apparently sympathetic one—and it is obvious the reporter writing the story has violated the established ground rules. If you made it clear that your comments were to be "off the record," and yet you were quoted by name, the journalist has committed a breach of trust that is almost unforgivable, even when he or she is on your side. A breach of confidence is simply not condoned in Washington. A journalist who would renege on a promise is a bad guy and should be dealt with accordingly.

In dealing with members of the press, one final rule is immutable: never condescend to them, even when they deserve it. Reporters are as dangerous as coiled cobras and will strike at the slightest suggestion of condescension. Better that you appear slightly flustered than megalomaniacal in their eyes.

Columnists

The above rules for dealing with reporters and determining whether a story is good or bad apply to news pieces. Opinion columns should be handled according to a slightly different set of rules. Columnists, despite their journalistic pretensions, are usually frustrated politicians. They don't report the news; they reduce their own prejudices to print. You should still expect them to observe journalistic ethics in protecting sources, but by definition they are not bound by the attributes of temperance and objectivity; they are expected to denounce various positions. They are wielders of poison pens restrained neither by fact nor good sense.

Due to their unique position within the fourth estate, you should feel free to lobby columnists just as you would congressmen or senators. You can even use many of the congressional lobbying tactics described in later chapters—for instance, you can plant stories with columnists much as you would insert statements into the *Congressional Record*.

However, no columnist—and few members of Congress—will kowtow to your every request simply because you agree with him or her. Columnists are invariably intelligent, sensitive, and egotistical. They will not merely reprint your views any more than a member of Congress would, but when honestly and forthrightly approached, columnists will welcome your assistance on a "no strings attached" basis.

A strongly worded column in support of your position is worth reprinting. Copies of opinion columns written by people who have no personal stake in the outcome of your campaign can be some of the most effective propaganda.

On the other hand, a column that opposes your position should not be judged by the same standards as a negative news piece. Readers generally know the prejudices of the columnists and expect them to take particular positions. Don't be too distressed if George Will, Robert Novak, or Charles Krauthammer roasts you, as long he doesn't accuse you of immoral, illegal, or unethical activities. A scathing column by a well-known opponent means you have attained credibility; you may be able to use it to your own advantage. For years,

Ralph Nader used to begin his speeches by saying, "As you know, General Motors doesn't like me much."

The Press Release

From time to time your group should issue press releases, if only to reestablish your identity with the media. The occasions for press releases are almost infinite, but some of the most common are as follows:

- issuance of a major policy statement
- reaction to a statement or action by the government or your opponents
- announcement of a press conference
- issuance of a study supporting your viewpoint by your group or some other group or agency
- announcement of major media events (e.g., demonstrations) sponsored by your group or an affiliated organization
- announcement of changes in the composition of your group (e.g., endorsement of your group's position by other organizations)
- announcement of major policy changes, endorsement of political candidates, or endorsement of the positions of other groups

Although opportunities for issuing press releases may seem endless, you should not overdo it. Releases should be issued only when there is a news peg to justify them, and few organizations have the news pegs available to justify a daily or even weekly press release. By their nature, releases should be irregular; this establishes their credibility and newsworthiness.

The press release should be carefully typed, free of errors, and written as if it were a news story you would like to see in print. Often, press releases are reprinted word for word in newspapers, particularly if they are picked up by the wire services. You cannot blame publications for bad press if you wrote the story yourself. Be sure that all press releases are double-spaced so they are easy to read and edit and that they contain at least the following elements:

- Date and time of release. If you wish to hold the release for a time later than the date you actually distribute it to the press, put the words "Embargoed for Release Until [Time/Date]" at the top of the page.

- ✦A dateline. This element should be placed at the beginning of the first paragraph of the release. It is not just the current date but the location from which the press release is issued (e.g., "March 3, Washington, D.C."). Note that if the release is to be embargoed until some point in the future, the dateline may be different than the date and time of release.

- ✦Notification, either in the letterhead or at the bottom of the release, that your group was responsible for preparing and issuing it.

- ✦The names and telephone numbers of individuals within your group from whom additional information may be obtained. Be sure to include e-mail addresses, cell phone numbers, etc. so reporters can contact them at any time—not just during working hours. Be sure you have briefed the persons to whom you have directed further inquiries.

Press releases should be cleared through a committee of your organization. No one individual should be given sole authority to prepare and issue releases. These are the public statements of your position. You will have to live with them for years to come. They are simply too important to be left to a single person's discretion.

A press release should be carried by hand to the Washington offices of the publications you wish to reach. Sending it through the mail is an acknowledgment of the lack of urgency of your release and will substantially diminish the chance that it will be picked up by the press. Releases by e-mail are often disregarded by the media; reporters are so inundated with e-mails that their electronic trashcans are full of them. In some cases, e-mail releases can work, but only if buttressed by telephone calls both in advance of and following the release. Most reporters maintain a "private" e-mail address for really important stuff (and messages from their friends). If you have this private address, send press releases there. You should also post the press release on your Web site.

Clipping Services

You have issued your press release and contacted reporters and columnists, but how do you know if your efforts have had an effect? One way to find out if your stories are being carried is by having a vast network of members willing to send you copies of stories that appear in their local newspapers; another is to search for news stories online; a third is to hire a professional clipping service. These services review hundreds of publications every day and will send you copies of articles regarding your issue for a fixed fee plus an additional charge per clipping. The articles will be sent to you on a daily or weekly basis, as you prefer, generally by e-mail. Clipping services can also monitor the broadcast media and send transcripts of stories carried by the networks and in some cases even local stations.

If media relations are an important part of your lobbying campaign, a clipping service may be a good way to double-check your effectiveness. It can be expensive, however, so content yourself with specifying merely a dozen or so publications to be reviewed. If a story has been picked up by the wire services, it will appear in virtually identical form in scores of papers. Seeing it in each publication will not do you much good; what's most significant is that the story made the wire services at all.

Far more efficient than a clipping service—and significantly cheaper—is to do a simple Google search using key words from your press releases and campaign. You should be able to get a pretty good idea of the scope of the coverage of your issue by the number of hits you get, and you should look carefully at some of the stories to see if the article was picked up by the wire services.

What If They Roast You?

You may review your coverage and find that the press is devastating. Half of the news outlets did not even print the story and those that did gave you either little or blatantly hostile coverage. What do you do?

There are only a few times in a lobbying campaign when humility is a virtue; this is one of them. Uniformly hostile press almost always indicates that you have not done your job. Either your position has no merit (which, for the purposes of this book, we presume to be false), or you have made substantial errors in your media campaign. To list all the mistakes you could have made would require a separate book, but we can review the most obvious ones:

+ Your project is not newsworthy. You may have approached the wrong publications or the wrong individuals at the wrong time.
+ Your method of reaching the press did not convey a sense of immediacy and relevance.
+ You or your group lack credibility for some reason.
+ Your timing in approaching the press was wrong; other more important news stories overwhelmed yours.

It is tempting to assume that your opponents had some influence with the press and squelched your story. Although you cannot expect your opposition to fight fair, a uniformly critical response is rarely the fault of some bogeyman. It may seem harsh to blame only yourself, but experience will teach you that this is generally the case. However, merely because you have had one or two setbacks with the media, don't be discouraged; it's part of the Washington game. Even presidential candidates have a tough time getting good press.

Letters to the Editor

One effective means of responding to hostile press is through the "Letters to the Editor" feature carried by most news outlets in both print and broadcast media. Most often the letters in these columns are reactions to previous stories or columns by the publication or station in question. In writing letters to the editor, abide by the following rules:

- Be brief. Letters to the editor rarely run over one hundred words or four column inches. All publications reserve the right to edit letters for clarity and length. If your letter is too long, it will be either rejected outright or so butchered as to be unrecognizable.

- If the writer is an officer of your group, it would be deceptive not to reveal that fact in the letter. Remember, your group's credibility is at stake. It can be undermined if you attempt some stunt such as attributing a letter to an apparently neutral party when in fact it is your own group's propaganda. If this deception is discovered by the media, you will lose more than you will gain.

- You are unlikely to be persuasive if your arguments are overly complex. Refer to only one issue in any letter to the editor, even if more than one subject was discussed in the news story or column to which you are responding.

- Restate the assertions in the original column or news story with which you disagree. You cannot assume that all the readers of your letter will have read the original article.

- Date and sign the letter; include your address and telephone number in case the editors want to confirm that you are actually the author of the letter before they publish it.

- If any letter to the editor purports to state the official position of your group, it should be cleared with at least two other members. As with press releases, your public positions are simply too important to entrust to the judgment of a single person.

If your letter is published, be sure to distribute copies, at least to members of your group.

Of all the aspects of lobbying considered in this book, press relations are covered most superficially. Reams have been written on the subject. Sometimes, following the basic ground rules regarding credibility, accessibility, and common sense is just not enough to secure the press coverage you need. You may want to consider retaining a public relations firm (see chapter 17). Since the media constitute the most powerful force outside the official government, public relations specialists may be an unfortunate necessity.

6

LETTERS TO THE HILL

"Politics is perhaps the only profession for which no preparation is thought necessary."

—Robert Louis Stevenson

One of the primary links between a member of Congress and the member's constituency is the mail. Each year, millions of letters arrive on Capitol Hill. Of this blizzard of paper, only a very small portion has a discernible impact upon the course of legislative events. Most of the balance is treated as junk mail by the various congressional offices; its receipt will be of no particular consequence to the congressman or senator. Of course, members of Congress would profess deep shock at this assertion. Almost every piece of mail, they will claim, is carefully examined and answered. Well, maybe, if you consider a three-second glance by an unpaid intern an "examination" and a form letter an "answer." The art of writing letters that make it through this routing process may be the difference between success and failure in your lobbying campaign.

Although e-mail, too, has become a very important communications medium, it still has a number of drawbacks, which will be discussed at the end of the chapter.

Short and Simple: Ask for Action

Although a letter to a member of Congress should be addressed to that member personally, there is not a single congressional office in which all mail addressed to the member automatically arrives on his or her desk. Invariably, mail arriving in an office will be routed through the staff. The only letters to reach the member will be those that the staff feels merit his or her attention.

One of the criteria they will use in deciding whether your letter is even seen by your congressman or senator is its length. Five-page, single-spaced letters almost never qualify for the member's attention. The best format is a regular business letter not exceeding two pages. Handwritten letters often receive special attention, particularly those written on the letterhead of a corporation or organization. The letter should be brief and to the point and should always include a request for action. The following elements should be included in most letters to the Hill:

1. brief description of your organization and its objectives

2. description of the issue

3. status of current law and/or pending legislation

4. effect of passage or defeat of legislation on the member of Congress's constituency

5. your group's position with regard to the issue

6. request for specific action on the member's part

7. reaffirmation of your group's interest in the member's position on this issue

A sample letter to a member of Congress might be as follows:

The Honorable Helen A. Toughnut
United States House of Representatives
Washington, DC 20515

Dear Congresswoman Toughnut:

On behalf of the members of Local 423 of the Flat Earth Society, I have been asked to inform you of a very serious issue that you will be voting on within the next few weeks. Our local is composed of 217 of your constituents, almost all of whom supported you in the last election. As you may recall, your reelection was the subject of a feature story in the Flat Earth News, a copy of which is attached for your consideration.

Our concern relates to H.R. 506, introduced by Congressman Undertow and currently pending in the Subcommittee on Elementary, Secondary, and Vocational Education of the Committee on Education and Labor. Section 171(b) of this bill would require compulsory instruction in Round Earth theory in all schools receiving federal funds. There is no provision for instruction of Flat Earth theory.

Over the years, our group has engaged in an intensive educational program within your district on the Flat Earth philosophy, and we believe that a significant minority, if not a majority, of your constituents acknowledge that the Earth is flat. In view of Congressman Undertow's bill, we have intensified our efforts to promote Flat Earthism.

We believe that Congressman Undertow's attempt to use government funds to promote his ill-conceived ideology represents an undermining of our strongly held beliefs and is a total waste of taxpayers' money. Although we recognize that you do not sit on the subcommittee in question, we hope you will make every effort to convince the committee chairman to shelve this legislation. We are, of course, prepared to testify at any public hearings that may be held to discuss this issue.

If this bill is allowed to pass, we would expect that, at the minimum, equal time be provided for instruction in Flat Earth theory at the elementary and secondary school levels.

For your consideration I have attached a fact sheet on the Undertow bill and a summary statement on Flat Earthism. As this is a matter of some urgency, we would appreciate hearing from you soon about your feelings on this subject. Please be assured that your comments will be distributed widely here in Bedrock County.

I am looking forward to hearing from you soon.

Sincerely,
Frank Bumknocker
Secretary
Local 423
Flat Earth Society

Names, Addresses, and Serial Numbers

A well-organized letter-writing campaign can be one of your most effective tools for influencing the outcome of legislation. In addition to the "organization" letter outlined above, individual members of your group should also be encouraged to write to key members of Congress. Using the list or spreadsheets you prepared in the action plan, you should prioritize letters from your members as follows:

1. letters to senators and congressmen in your members' state or district who have direct legislative influence over your issue (e.g., members of the committees considering pending legislation)

2. letters to other senators and congressmen in your members' state or district

3. letters to other senators and congressmen who serve on the relevant committees, but with whom your members do not have constituent relationships

4. letters to any other senator or congressman

One of the most fundamental errors that organizations make in grassroots letter-writing campaigns is to try to reach everyone on the Hill. There are 535 members of Congress; it is extremely unlikely you will be able to have all your members write to every congressman and senator. Depending upon the status of the legislation with which you are concerned, you should focus on the narrowest possible group, whether it be individual congressmen, subcommittee members, full committee members, or caucuses.

If a bill has been introduced recently, it will be referred automatically to a committee and subsequently to a subcommittee. Although there are exceptions, most subcommittees do not have more than twenty members, and some have as few as five or six. It is the subcommittee members who should be the first target of your letter-writing campaign. You will need the support of a congressional leader in any lobbying campaign, and a subcommittee member, particularly if he or she is of the majority party, can be indispensable. See if any members of your group have direct constituent relationships with any of the subcommittee members. These relationships are particularly useful if the subcommittee member in question is already inclined to be sympathetic to your position.

If the legislation has already been reported out of subcommittee, or if it is likely that it will be reported out, your next line of offense (or defense) is the full committee. Since the full committee will have many more members, it is much more likely that your members will have direct constituent relationships with at least one or two of them. Concentrate your efforts on their offices, and work with friendly staffers to determine the best tactics.

Since legislation must go through an identical procedure in both the House and the Senate, you have four opportunities to focus your campaign before the issue goes before the full House or Senate. On the House side, you will have an additional opportunity. Almost all bills are routed through the Rules Committee, which acts as a traffic cop for legislation, assigning priorities for debate and establishing rules for floor consideration. This is a small but influential committee; if you can take advantage of any direct constituent relationships here, you should.

If your issue requires the expenditure of federal funds, you will get yet another chance to present your case. In both the House and the Senate, virtually all revenue measures must be considered both by the committee with jurisdiction over the subject matter (e.g., Agriculture, Banking and Currency) and by the Appropriations Committee and its relevant subcommittees. The targeting procedure used with regular committees can also be used with the Appropriations Committee.

In addition, many bills affect more than one committee's jurisdiction. For example, a bill concerning water policy might be considered by the Agriculture and the Interior committees of both the House and the Senate. Be particularly alert to this. Some of your strongest supporters may serve on one committee and be unaware that relevant legislation is pending in another committee.

Form Letters Are Weighed, Not Read

A clear majority of all the mail received in a congressional office consists of preprinted post cards, form letters, and handwritten letters with identical wording. Promoters of this type of letter-writing campaign must have incredibly low estimation of the intelligence of congressional staffers. The person charged with opening and routing mail in a congressional office needs to see only three or four identical letters before he or she starts putting them in the junk mail category. The writers of such letters will get a form letter in return. It is almost a certainty that the member of Congress will never see such communications.

Because form-letter campaigns are so common, the Hill has developed an extremely sophisticated method for dealing with them. When a form letter arrives in the office of a member of Congress, the usual reaction of the low-level staff member is to say, "Give this guy a 44-B response." The "44-B response" is code for a form letter prepared by the member's staff for a particular type of letter. More sophisticated offices will even have individual paragraphs coded and the staffer might say, "Give these characters a 43-C first paragraph, 16-D second, and sign off with a 26-F."

The more personal your letter, the less likely the congressional office will be able to adapt its form response. Because of this, you can test a member's responsiveness to your letters and attention to your issue by analyzing his or her reply. If your original letter identifies specific individuals, issues, and organizations, you can usually tell whether the member or the member's staffers have given it attention by noting whether their answer makes direct reference to those specifics. If not, it is likely you were merely fed "into the bin." The more conscientious the member and the more effective his or her staff, the less likely you are to receive a form letter.

In sum, it is a waste of money to engage in a war of computers. Your form letters will be answered by form letters and you can be absolutely sure that the Hill's computers are better than yours. Any suggestion that your organization engage in a form letter or postcard blizzard should almost automatically be dismissed as a waste of time and money.

The Fact Sheet

The heart of an effective letter-writing campaign is apparent spontaneity. Members of your organization should write to members of Congress in their own words. They should be encouraged to include personal anecdotes. Misspellings, grammatical errors, etc., are not important. The only things that count are that they wrote and that the facts contained in their letters are accurate. To assure that your members write, it is often helpful to provide them with paper, pens, and stamped envelopes at a meeting and have them write out letters at that time. If this is logistically difficult, pleas to your members through your newsletter with telephone and e-mail follow-ups are often effective.

The only written material you should provide your members with is a three- or four-page fact sheet that outlines the facts of the particular issues and your position. *Never* give a sample letter to the members of your group. You should encourage your members to select one or two of the issues contained in your fact sheet and concentrate on them rather than merely rehashing all of the subjects it covers. Selection of issues should be left to the individual writing the letter. This will ensure even greater spontaneity. Your members should be cautioned not to send a copy of the fact sheet with their letter. This will destroy the spontaneity of the response and diminish the effectiveness of the overall campaign.

The purpose of the fact sheet is to make sure your members do not make unsubstantiated claims that could damage your group's credibility. It should contain the following:

1. statement of the issue
2. statement of your group's position
3. status of proposed legislation or administrative action
4. list of reasons to support (or oppose) pending legislation or administrative action
5. proposed action you wish the member of Congress to take

In addition, although it may prove difficult for you as the coordinator to personalize the fact sheet for each congressional district in which you have members, you should point out some local issues that your members may be unaware of—for instance, the position of their district's congressman.

Unless your group's members are very sophisticated, the wording of the fact sheet should be relatively simple. If your members would not be expected to have an intimate knowledge of congressional procedures, do not include anything in your fact sheet that would give the impression that they have been coached. A sample fact sheet for an average membership might read as follows:

Fact Sheet on H.R. 506:
Round Earth Amendments

Congressman Sinkum Undertow (R-N.J.) has recently introduced a bill (H.R. 506) that would amend the Comprehensive Educational Curriculum Act of 1954. This legislation would provide for mandatory instruction in Round Earth theory in all elementary and secondary schools that receive any federal funds.

The bill would undermine Flat Earth dogma and is a waste of taxpayers' money. The Flat Earth Society strongly opposes this legislation.

The bill is currently pending in the Committee on Education and Labor in the United States House of Representatives and may come to a vote at any time. Our congresswoman, Helen Toughnut, has supported fairness in presenting Flat Earth philosophy, but it is likely the vote on this issue will be extremely close. The Undertow bill should be defeated for the following reasons:

+ Millions of taxpayer dollars would be wasted in requiring teachers to undergo Round Earth training so that they could effectively promote this philosophy. This is not a legitimate government function and should at best be paid for by those groups promoting Round Earthism.

+ Children are already subjected to all sorts of propaganda ranging from television commercials to comic books to spam on the Internet; the government should not subsidize additional propaganda.

+ Round Earth theory flies in the face of the beliefs of many patriotic Americans who embrace the Flat Earth theory and who, as parents, do not feel it appropriate that their beliefs be contradicted by teachers who are paid at taxpayer expense.

+ Flat Earth theory is accepted by scores of learned men and women and is at least as valid as Round Earth theory. It is highly discriminatory to promote one belief over the other.

+ The Flat Earth issue is fundamental. Many people will base their votes for members of Congress only on this issue.

- Round Earthism is being promoted by a fringe element that does not represent the mainstream of American thought.
- Mandatory instruction in Round Earthism would require additional expenditure of local funds, eroding the tax base for public schools at a time when inflation should be one of our primary concerns.
- The Undertow bill would create a huge federal bureaucracy, which is neither needed nor wanted by the American people.

The fact sheet should be sent with a cover letter to all of your members, which should also give the complete names and addresses of members of Congress to whom you wish your members to write. The cover letter can have a somewhat more political tone than the fact sheet. A sample might be as follows:

Dear Fellow Flat Earth Supporter:

As you know, Congressman Undertow has introduced legislation that would institutionalize the teaching of Round Earth theory in the public schools. This legislation would be devastating to our cause and would cost millions of tax dollars. I hope you will write to your own congressman and senators immediately and express your opposition to the Undertow bill. For your convenience I have attached a fact sheet on this legislation. It is designed to give you some direction in preparing your letter, but your letter should be personal. Do not send the fact sheet itself to the congressman or senator.

Please also write to the following members of Congress, who will have great influence on this legislation:

The Honorable Sam C. Slackman
United States Senate
Washington, DC 20510

The Honorable Billy K. Butterball
United States House of Representatives
Washington, DC 20515

The Honorable Gladys Tiltmeyer
United States House of Representatives
Washington, DC 20515

The Honorable Thurbridge D. Silverstein
United States Senate
Washington, DC 20510

Please send us a copy of the letter you send to these members of Congress, as well as copies of any responses you receive. We will keep you posted on our progress.

Sincerely,
Paris Ritz
Secretary
Local 34

The fact sheet and cover letter should go out as early as possible during the course of the lobbying campaign. It usually takes some time for your members to get around to writing.

Following Up

As the coordinator of a lobbying campaign, you will have to follow up both with your own members and with the Hill. During the course of the letter-writing campaign, almost everyone in your organization will promise to write, but very few actually do. About a week after you send the request to your members, call them to inquire whether they have written their letters. One of the best ways to tell if your people have actually written to their congressional delegations is to persistently ask them to give you copies of their original letters or the responses from the Hill. (You will need samples of the latter in any event, to measure the effect your letter-writing campaign is having.) You must actively seek a reputation as a nag if your letter-writing campaign is to be successful.

The second aspect of following up is with the Hill itself. You should get sample copies of the types of letters that individual congressional offices are sending back to your members. They will give you a good idea of where the members of Congress actually stand on your issue—who your supporters and opponents are. Pay particular attention to letters that suggest a general sympathy with your cause but state that the member cannot vote on your side on this particular issue. If a member takes this position, he or she may be a prime candidate for follow-up meetings in which you could discuss facts or answer questions about your issue.

If the responses include congressional critiques of your position, they may give you an idea of what kind of adjustments you should make in your lobbying campaign—particularly if your views are misunderstood by a significant number of respondents. These critiques can also help you detect whether your opponents have been active. If the same objections or statistics appear in a number of negative responses, it's likely that your opponents have provided the information. It is incumbent upon you to rebut them.

If a response from a particular member of Congress includes facts, statistics, etc., that are simply erroneous, you should immediately draft a very polite response including the correct information and inviting the member to contact your organization for additional data. This draft response should be sent to the person who originally contacted the member of Congress and that person—not you—should forward it to the appropriate congressional office. A sample of such a letter might read as follows:

Dear Senator Belfry:

Thank you very much for your rapid response to my letter of September 5. I can certainly appreciate your position and would probably adopt it as my own if the facts were as you stated them. You noted, for example, that only federally supported elementary schools (e.g., schools for military dependents) would be affected by the proposed Round Earth Bill. In fact, virtually every school in the country that receives any federal assistance for such programs as hot lunches, etc., would be required to comply with the Round Earth instruction legislation.

This means, in effect, that over 95 percent of all schools in the United States (excluding only the rare private school that receives absolutely no federal funding) would be required to comply with this federal directive. In effect, the school board here in Columbus County would not be permitted to control the curriculum of our own schools. This is a problem of immediate concern to us and not merely a philosophical consideration. This being the case, I hope you might reconsider your tentative support of this legislation and let me know how you feel.

If you need any additional information on this measure, I would be pleased to provide it for you; or, if you prefer, your staff can contact Ms. Cynthia Winetroup, our legislative representative in Washington. She can be reached at (202) 555-0123.

Thank you again for your interest and courtesy.

Sincerely,
Rebecca Moss

If a particular member of Congress continues to oppose your cause even after you have corrected his or her errors, it would probably be a waste of time and energy to continue the correspondence. If the individual is critical to the passage or defeat of the legislation, it might be worth your time to pay his or her office a personal visit, but endless correspondence is rarely productive, particularly since the member is probably not drafting the letters personally. You should find out which staffer is putting these words in the member's mouth and speak with that person directly.

Some congressional offices are more efficient than others, and it is not unusual for smaller offices to be overwhelmed with correspondence. If a particular member of Congress does not respond to your letters within two to three weeks, it is advisable to send a second letter; mention the first correspondence and again request an answer. Some offices have adopted a policy of responding only to letters originating within their congressional district or state. Therefore, personal visits may be required at some point.

A letter-writing campaign can be enormously effective if it is properly administered. As with all of the aspects of lobbying, however, a letter-writing campaign involves a lot of work—not just political clout.

E-mail

Given how cheap and easy it is to send e-mails these days, many groups have tried to flood the Hill with electronic messages. But congressional offices hate spam as much as you do, and they employ sophisticated spam filters to detect and delete mass mailings. In addition, almost all congressional offices now ask for your name, e-mail address, and nine-digit ZIP code before they will allow you to send an e-mail. This way, they can limit their reading to mail coming directly from constituents. Of course, you can lie about your ZIP code to get through, but looking for authorized ZIP codes is tedious, and gaining access through deceit is dangerous. You are trying to build trust in your group and credibility for your cause. Fibbing here hardly enhances your chances of persuading the member of the righteousness of your ways.

Most offices also require that you specify the general topic of your note before they will allow you to send it. Some even require that you solve a simple math problem, to ensure that a real person and not a mass e-mail computer program is seeking access. Finally, many offices have very tight rules against attachments, rightly fearing attempts by hackers to disrupt their systems. The overall result is that it's often no easier to reach a member electronically than through conventional mail.

Even if you do decide to try an e-mail campaign, be sure you follow all of the rules outlined above for regular snail mail. In particular, do not encourage your members to merely cut and paste a form letter to their members of Congress. The staffer who opens these will quickly see a pattern and generate a form letter back to your members. The substance of your message will be lost in the process. Trying to overwhelm congressional offices with electronic messages is a fool's errand. Again, their technology is better than yours, and your efforts will be wasted.

Of course, all offices have numerous e-mail boxes, most of which are confidential. If you are fortunate enough to gain access to a staffer's personal e-mail account, for example, do not abuse it. Use it *only* for sending (very short) notes to the staffer—not long epistles. *Do not* share the staffer's e-mail addresses with anyone. If the staffer starts getting unsolicited stuff from someone not in his or her personal address book, it will generally wind up in the trash. Worse yet, the staffer may change e-mail addresses and your back-channel means of communication may be lost.

E-mailing has obvious advantages over conventional mail in terms of cost and speed. Its primary disadvantage is that individual messages are so often lost in the deluge of electronic messages received on the Hill each day. Because of this, real letters from real people receive more attention than even the most meticulously planned e-mail campaign. An e-mail campaign may give you greater flexibility, but try the old way as well. The two forms of communication often work best in tandem.

7

DEMONSTRATIONS

"The object of oratory alone is not truth, but persuasion."

—Lord Macaulay

Demonstrations or Lobbying?

Demonstrations, though sometimes necessary, are rarely the most effective or desirable means of communicating your group's views to the Congress. The chanting of slogans by faceless bodies is hardly the essence of rational debate. For example, environmentalists have largely abandoned mass demonstrations as their primary tool and have developed sophisticated networks of citizen lobbyists to influence legislation. Their effectiveness has been manifest: literally hundreds of laws have been adopted in the past decade that protect everything from native grasses in Kansas to air quality in the Everglades. Similarly, your members can be infinitely more effective if they walk the halls of the Congress rather than the streets of Washington. One hundred lobbyists, if properly motivated and trained, can be much more powerful than one thousand demonstrators.

The only circumstances in which demonstrations might be more effective than face-to-face lobbying are when you have minimal control of your own group or when supporting organizations are committed to your goals but you have no control whatsoever over their activities. In such cases it is sometimes better to keep them away from members of Congress; they may do more to confuse the issue than to clarify it. When you don't know what your so-called supporters may do, a demonstration might be best.

If you decide that a demonstration is the safest route, make sure you do it right. There are four general rules to follow if you are planning a demonstration:

1. Recognize that the demonstration is as much for the benefit of your own supporters as it is to convince the Congress of the rectitude of your views.

Demonstrations can build a feeling of solidarity within your organization and encourage your members to commit themselves to your group's objectives. A Washington demonstration is a political pep rally.

2. Understand that demonstrations are media events designed to draw public attention to your issue. If you ignore this aspect of demonstrations, you may as well tell your people to stay home. If your demonstration is to be effective, the media must be carefully apprised of your plans. The mere fact that you are having a demonstration or rally will not necessarily excite the press. You must also provide newsworthy events, in the form of either gimmicks or well-known public speakers.

3. Since the news media are an integral part of your demonstration, don't allow too many of your warts to show. A noisy demonstration is one thing; an unruly one is another. Reporters are always alert to newsworthy events, and massive arrests are certainly newsworthy. It is rarely beneficial to encourage or even tolerate disruptive activity.

4. Because demonstrations are media events, be as visual as possible. Flags, posters, and picket signs are de rigueur in any Washington demonstration. You should not, however, encourage the display or chanting of obviously anti-American symbols or slogans. An anarchist flag will alienate many observers who might otherwise be sympathetic to your cause. Symbols are indeed powerful, and they should be carefully chosen. The peace symbol developed in the early 1950s is a perfect example. It incorporates the semaphore "N.D."—the initials of "nuclear disarmament." This symbol, though it obviously does not convey a neutral sentiment, has attained credibility far removed from radicalism.

Within the context of these general rules, successful demonstrations have a number of other hallmarks.

Invite Celebrity Speakers

Since a demonstration is designed to reach many more people than just the participants, it is always a good idea to have a celebrity speaker at your rally. Be it a movie star, a member of Congress, a trade union official, or even a noted pediatrician, a name speaker at your demonstration will not only help attract press attention but also increase the number of demonstrators as well.

Celebrities often have enormous egos, so you should brief them fully on the objectives of your demonstration as well as on who else will appear. You should also suggest issues that may not be covered by other speakers. They may not follow your precise recommendations, but you should still give them the party line.

In the same vein, it is sometimes desirable to enlist politically committed celebrities to provide entertainment—for instance, instrumental or singing groups. The goal is more to increase the size of your demonstration than to impress the general public. Often, such groups will appear for free or at a greatly reduced rate. They should be approached through their agents well in advance of the proposed demonstration.

Media Relations

You cannot expect a demonstration to receive adequate press coverage if you do not include media representatives in virtually every phase of your planning. You should issue a series of press releases prior to your demonstration detailing the logistics and objectives of your program. Never publicly state that one of your objectives is to achieve media attention. Obvious exploitation is a turnoff to the press.

As the time for the demonstration nears, you should distribute more press releases and hold more press conferences; the turnout for your demonstration depends in large measure on the amount of newsprint, airtime, blog references, and e-mail buzz it has generated. The more media hype you can create, the more demonstrators you will have. The only way you will generate hype is through constant communication with the very people who are in turn tacitly promoting attendance at your rallies. The more contact you have with the press, the more likely it is you will receive the coverage necessary to make your rally a success.

When estimating the number of demonstrators you expect, however, be conservative. The press relish reporting that only a fraction of the predicted number turned out for a particular demonstration—but they also love to report that a demonstration exceeded the planners' initial projections.

Signs and Symbols

As noted previously, symbols are an extremely effective method of political communication. They can convey a philosophy far more quickly than can rhetoric. If possible, your group should design its own symbol for use in demonstrations, one that will evoke sympathy or at least understanding.

You should avoid incorporating existing radical symbols into yours. Raised fists or guns, defaced logos, and red stars leave the majority of Americans with a negative impression. You do not want to alienate potential allies by using loaded signs or symbols; rather, you want to develop an identity of your own. The United Farm Workers' eagle is an example of a brilliantly conceived and executed symbol, recognizable to millions of Americans. It is a statement by itself and makes no reference to other political ideologies.

Once you have adopted a symbol, it will become known only if it is used frequently and conspicuously. It should be displayed prominently at all rallies and demonstrations and carried on picket signs, T-shirts, and any other promotional materials you create.

Timing

Good weather is often critical to a demonstration's success. Few but the absolutely committed will march down Pennsylvania Avenue in a thunderstorm. Luckily, weather in Washington is very predictable. Winters are gray and moist; temperatures rarely fall below 25°F. Spring (late March to mid-May) is beautiful, with temperatures in the mid-70s most of the time, but there are frequent showers. Summer (through mid-September) is very hot and humid. Autumn is the best time of year for demonstrations; the evenings are cool, humidity is low, and any rain is easily predictable. All other factors being equal, a demonstration held in late September or early October would offer the best possibility for a good turnout. If you must hold a demonstration at another time of the year and are expecting many participants from outside the Washington area, be sure to warn them about the Washington climate and advise them to dress appropriately.

When planning your demonstration you should also be sensitive to the schedule of the Congress. In August, senators and congressmen are back in their home states and districts mending political fences; a rally held at that time will rarely attract much congressional attention. In election years, the Congress breaks for the Republican and Democratic conventions in the summer and takes an extended leave of absence for the campaign starting in mid-September. In an off-year election cycle (i.e., one that does not include a presidential race), members generally leave town for the entire month of October. Other traditional congressional holidays include Memorial Day, Labor Day, Christmas, Jefferson's and Washington's birthdays, and Easter.

Also vital to the timing of your demonstration is the relative availability of your members. Many organizations rely on young people to fill out their demonstrations. If this is the case with your group, demonstrations during Thanksgiving and college spring breaks are a good idea. For family-oriented issues, weekends when working parents are available are best. Warmer months are preferred for campaigns directed toward the needs of the elderly.

Your demonstration should also be timed to coincide with a major "breakpoint" in public policy. Such breakpoints can include

1. a vote on the Senate or House floor on legislation affecting your issue
2. a previously announced decision date by the administration on an issue affecting your group
3. anniversary dates commemorating events significant to your organization

Momentum, a much vaguer consideration than those listed above, is another important factor in the timing of demonstrations. When public interest in your campaign is on the rise, a demonstration can serve both to maintain it and to fuel its fires.

Appeal to Justice

Many demonstrators believe they can achieve their objectives through the shock value of silly, iconoclastic charades. For instance, the almost annual demonstrations against the World Bank generally include huge papier-mâché puppets portraying international bankers as blood-sucking parasites or worse. Although such antics may make the evening news, they rarely impress policy makers. People react more favorably to perceived injustices than to insults; your demonstration is more likely to stir up sympathy if it frames your cause as fundamentally just. Thus you should focus your demonstration on your objections to being treated unfairly. A good example of this technique can be found in the abortion rights movement. This group characterizes itself as supporting "freedom of choice" instead of claiming to be "proabortion."

Avoid Zealotry

During the course of any lobbying campaign and particularly during demonstrations, there is always a temptation to get carried away by the mood of the moment. Emotionalism is fine, but it cannot be allowed to override common sense. Intemperate comments can harm your campaign if they don't really convey what you mean.

This is not to suggest that strident words do not have a place in a demonstration—they do. A dispassionate demonstration is not very exciting to attend or to watch. There is a narrow line, however, between justified emotion and mindless fanaticism. A good partisan speech can easily turn into the frantic ramblings of a demagogue. There is no guide to help you distinguish between the two other than common sense.

You can, however, do something about the fanatics in your own camp. If you know in advance that some demonstrators are extremist, you can keep them segregated from the rest of your troops. For example, in the later demonstrations of the Vietnam-era antiwar movement, those committed to the cause of North Vietnam were carefully isolated from the more moderate demonstrators. Under no circumstances should you permit extremists to share the podium with rational adherents to your cause. Reporters are delighted by uninhibited rhetoric and your entire campaign, no matter how defensible, may rise or fall on the ravings of these fringe elements.

Dealing with the Police

No matter how careful your planning, in large demonstrations you will have to deal with the police. In Washington, this sometimes means coordinating your activities with at least four different police forces. Washington has, at last count, fourteen different constabularies. The four most prominent police agencies with which you will have to deal are the Metropolitan Police Department (MPD), the Capitol Police, the Park Police, and the Executive Protective Service (the uniformed branch of the Secret Service).

Contrary to popular mythology, the Washington police agencies are generally professional and cooperative—and sometimes even have a sense of humor. They are so accustomed to demonstrations that it is extremely difficult to provoke them. Many groups have come to Washington expecting confrontations— even hoping for them—only to be disappointed by the courtesy of the cops. It is highly unlikely that you will be able to characterize the authorities here as "fascist pigs" as credibly as you might in other cities. Thus, outright confrontation with the police is not likely to get you good press and should be avoided.

All four agencies noted above have community relations departments designed to assist you in planning and carrying out your demonstration. The departments will not only help you establish parade routes, but also provide police protection rather than harassment. They will help you train your marshals and will cooperate with them during the demonstration itself. They can make your demonstration orderly, suppress violent opposition, clear streets for your group, and even help you make sure such necessities as toilet facilities are available. In short, you cannot afford not to cooperate with the police. If you plan to have a demonstration, do not fail to contact them well in advance.

Community Relations

Washington has endured so many demonstrations that the reactions of its residents are almost unique: they don't take them too seriously. They tend to regard them as one of the hazards of living in the nation's capital. This attitude can change for the worse or the better, however, if the demonstration either generates substantial inconvenience on one hand or is a conscious attempt to promote goodwill in the city on the other.

A perfect example of both occurred some years ago. At one point, farmers from the American Agriculture Movement were almost literally run out of town for driving their tractors up and down the Mall, destroying the shrubbery and buckling the sidewalks. A short time later they were greeted as saviors for bringing those same tractors to snowbound streets and rescuing stranded motorists. Neither action had much to do with their issue, but they left with more goodwill than when they entered. Remember, many Washingtonians are lobbyists, congressional staff members, and bureaucrats. If your group can attract their attention in a positive way—even if it has nothing to do with your policy objectives—you are well ahead of the game.

Washington is a city with all the ills of most urban areas and, as such, it presents many opportunities for community relations projects. Virtually any such project your group undertakes will get attention, which cannot help but benefit your organization. For example, if your group advocates clean water, a symbolic cleanup of the Potomac River would ensure not only good press but also community sympathy. A visit to a local abortion clinic might engender good press for both pro- and antiabortion groups. The possibilities are endless. Even if the community relations project is only tangentially related to your primary issue, the people on the Hill who matter will take note. One hundred demonstrators cleaning up an inner-city alley will receive as much coverage as the same number of demonstrators getting arrested. It may seem callous to suggest that community projects should be done for the purpose of public relations, but it is shocking that more groups do not recognize the value of this tactic.

Logistics

It is easy enough to announce a demonstration in Washington; it is something else to actually have one. There are hundreds of details with which you must concern yourself. A few of them are as follows:

Permits

If you plan even a small demonstration, you must secure permits from the city as well as the federal government. For information regarding required permits, contact the police agencies noted above.

Housing

Washington has one of the highest hotel-room-to-resident ratios of any city in the country. Nevertheless, adequate housing is always at a premium, particularly during the spring and summer. Camping out is not a viable option in the immediate vicinity of Washington, so you should be sure all demonstrators have shelter during their stay in Washington. If hotel space is unavailable or is too expensive for your group, there are numerous organizations—churches, for instance—that may be able to offer temporary housing.

Transportation

Buses are the traditional method of bringing demonstrators to Washington, and within the city there is an excellent transportation system. Buses stop regularly in all parts of the city, and a subway—the Metro—provides rapid access to Capitol Hill and the downtown area. You may want to consider housing your demonstrators near the terminus of the subway lines, where housing rates are cheaper.

Miscellaneous

To be effective, a demonstration must have adequate posters, sound systems, sanitary facilities, food, and other necessities. Although such accommodations may seem obvious, you would be surprised at how many demonstration organizers forget that people need to eat, the result being demonstrators scattered over a twenty-block area searching for hot dogs when they should be at a rally. You must pay as much attention to the needs of your demonstrators as you do to the specifics of your issue.

In large demonstrations, it is imperative you provide first-aid services. Invariably, a number of demonstrators will be injured or suffer from heat prostration or more severe maladies.

You should also be alert to various fundraising possibilities: selling food to hungry demonstrators or selling buttons, banners, T-shirts, and other paraphernalia related to your cause. If this sounds mercenary, remember, both Oral Roberts and Abbie Hoffman advocated the same tactics. A demonstration is a kind of carnival; there is no political or ethical rule that prohibits you from using it to gain additional funds to promote your position.

8

THE CONGRESSIONAL HEARING

"Laws are like cobwebs, which may catch small flies, but let wasps and hornets break through."

—Jonathan Swift

Another way to get exposure for your group is to testify at congressional hearings. These hearings are held by Senate and House committees and subcommittees and are almost always open to the public. As such, they provide a good vehicle for increasing your public recognition.

What Are Congressional Hearings?

Congressional hearings are an essential part of the legislative process. There are two basic types: legislative hearings and oversight hearings. Legislative hearings are by far the more common. They are held to consider bills that have been introduced by members of Congress and referred to the committee and subcommittee concerned with the issue. Legislative hearings are usually announced well in advance, and the chairman of the committee or subcommittee will request the views of the administration as well as those of other interested parties. These hearings may last from a few hours to several days, as in the case of appropriations bills.

Oversight hearings, on the other hand, are generally held to review the effectiveness of existing legislation. They are usually called when there is some obvious problem with the enforcement of a statute, and they tend to focus on the executive branch; the Watergate hearings could be characterized as oversight hearings. Often the Government Accountability Office (GAO) is called to testify regarding its investigation of the executive agency or department charged with acting improperly or failing to act. The agency or department being investigated is almost always called to defend its record, and there is usually an opportunity for the public at large to present their views. Although this type of hearing may well be the more important, the time spent on congressional oversight is far exceeded by that devoted to new legislation.

Although there is a practical difference between oversight and legislative hearings, this distinction is not raised to the level of law or parliamentary procedure as far as members of Congress are concerned. To them, a hearing is a hearing; any issue relevant to the general subject matter under consideration may be taken up. It is not unheard-of for new legislation to actually be drafted in the middle of an oversight hearing.

How to Have a Congressional Hearing Scheduled

With notable exceptions, very few legislative measures are enacted into law without hearings, so scheduling is critically important. During any legislative session, less than one-quarter of the bills introduced ever receive consideration in hearings. If all bills received the attention of a full-scale hearing, the Congress would have to either double its membership or be involved in committee action 24 hours a day, 365 days a year.

Often a number of bills will be considered in the same hearing, but only one or two will actually receive serious attention; the balance will be shunted aside or ignored. Hearings held just prior to adjournment, particularly during election years, are likely to lead nowhere; there will be no time for the full House or Senate to adequately consider the proposals, even if they are affirmatively reported out of committee. If you are supporting a particular measure, it is critically important to secure thorough hearings early in the legislative session.

Securing early hearings, like much of the art of lobbying, is not as simple as it first appears. The scheduling is entirely up to the discretion of the committee or subcommittee chairman. Unless your measure is cosponsored by the chairman or is an "administration bill" submitted by the executive branch, hearings are not automatic. The chairman must be convinced that there is considerable congressional interest in your measure.

While it is not essential that the chairman be one of your allies, his or her active opposition severely reduces your chances of success. It is, therefore, advisable to approach the chairman early in the game, preferably shortly after the legislation has been introduced. This should be done using the same method as with other staff contacts (see chapter 11). You should also ask your other congressional supporters to contact the chairman and request hearings. If you encounter intractable resistance from the committee chairman, you should consult your other congressional allies and determine whether the measure might be considered in another committee, or whether it could be reported out of committee through parliamentary maneuvers, which have been successfully employed with many controversial measures. Going over the chairman's head is unusual, but in certain circumstances it may be your only hope.

Even when the chairman is not overtly hostile, hearing schedules often slip. You must be constantly vigilant against the institutional procrastination of the Hill.

On the other hand, if you are opposing a particular piece of legislation, one of your first tactics should be to delay committee hearings on the measure. Since every committee on the Hill is extremely jealous of what it considers its territory, contact your sources within other committees to which the legislation might have been referred and suggest to them that a different committee is handling matters that rightfully should be considered by them. You can often get consecutive or concurrent referral of the bill. Even if it passes in one committee, you can bottle it up in another.

How to Be Invited to Testify at a Congressional Hearing

Outside Washington, testimony at congressional hearings conjures up images of klieg lights, TV cameras, and instant fame (or infamy). Although that is sometimes the case, it is highly unlikely you would want such hoopla at your hearing.

The press, particularly the broadcast media, cover congressional hearings thoroughly only when the scent of scandal is in the air. To get major network news involved, there must have been a massive foul-up somewhere. For that reason, the most widely covered congressional hearings are oversight rather than legislative hearings. So unless you are an expert in media manipulation, don't try to make your name in an oversight hearing. Stick to legislative hearings your first time out.

Most congressional hearings are pretty tame by Hollywood standards, and it is not difficult to be invited to testify if you play your cards right. Once you have been successful in getting a hearing date, talk to the staff members who serve both your congressional allies and the committee. You should make it clear to them that you are eager to testify at the hearings and that you are prepared to keep your testimony short. As an added inducement, it is sometimes a good idea to hint that a well-known spokesperson of your cause will be the person who actually testifies. This is particularly useful if the spokesperson is an important constituent of members of the committee.

If the price of being permitted to testify is to have a celebrity do the talking, there are a number of practical rules to follow. If celebrity spokespeople are well known enough to impress the Hill, it is probable the press will also pick up their remarks, and these celebrities will not always be as well briefed as their Washington representatives (or you). Never allow them to speak extemporaneously before a congressional committee. Sometimes, celebrity advocates can undo weeks of work with a few simple, stupid statements. They can undermine carefully refined positions if they are unfamiliar with the facts and your efforts. Worst of all, if their testimony departs in any significant respect from the information you have already given the Hill, your entire group's credibility can be damaged or destroyed. If you bring in one or more uninformed celebrity to testify, be sure to write their testimony, and don't let them depart from it. You should also personally accompany them to the witness table and be prepared to kick them in the shins if they start ad-libbing. Celebrity witnesses are an excellent way to be sure your group is permitted to testify, but they can cause extreme embarrassment if they are not fully apprised of the facts and your position.

In addition to orally requesting an opportunity to testify, you should also send a formal written request to the committee and subcommittee chairmen, observing any deadline date specified by the committee itself.

The Statement

In almost all congressional hearings, you will have two opportunities to present your views: an extensive written statement and live testimony. Both will be included in the record. It is never a good idea to merely prepare a four-to-five-page speech and then read it at a congressional hearing. This is condescending and insulting, particularly since most committees require you to submit twenty or so copies of your written statement in advance. If you insist on reading your testimony, be prepared to catch glimpses of committee members reading other material, checking the latest stock market quotations, or telling jokes to their colleagues while you testify.

Your written statement should contain a detailed analysis of your position. Depending upon the issue, it can be twenty or more pages long (but never more than thirty). Generally, this document will be read in detail only by congressional staffers; in unusual circumstances it can provide backup for a member of Congress who becomes actively interested in your subject. It can include graphs, charts, and other data that would be difficult to read into the record. Your written statement should be very carefully proofed.

Most committees require that the written statement be submitted two to three days in advance of the actual hearing. You should carefully check the specific requirements of the relevant committee to determine the number of copies required and try to meet the deadline. Since all witnesses must submit their statements at the same time, you may be able to get a sneak preview of what your opposition will be saying prior to the hearing. However, many people, including the press, will have the same idea, and staffs are usually reluctant to part with advance copies of statements; to persuade them, you will have to have developed your staff contacts well. Even if you are unable to get advance copies of all testimony prior to the hearings, you should at least be able to secure the statements of those organizations sympathetic to your cause. Repetitive statements by several groups on the same issue rarely accomplish much; your appearance will be much more effective if you and your allies can mount a coordinated presentation. Even if your written testimony overlaps, you can often prevent redundancies in your oral statements.

On the day of the hearing, you should bring another twenty-five to thirty copies of your written statement to place on the press table, where other witnesses, members of the press, and spectators can pick up copies. Although the original filing with the committee is supposed to take care of such needs, it almost never does. If you expect to be given adequate exposure by the media, this should be considered more than a mere courtesy. Most news stories are prepared from the written statement and not the oral testimony at hearings.

Your oral testimony, unlike your written statement, should not be distributed to the committee prior to the hearing. In fact, it should not be transcribed at all. Your preparations should consist primarily of notes or a typed summary of the most important points you want to make. Your testimony should contain numerous references to your written statement, but it should not attempt to incorporate all the points you have made in writing. It should be dramatic. You want to have the committee's attention, but you will not get it if you merely repeat what you have already written in your prepared statement. Despite all the dictates of common sense, most witnesses at congressional hearings insist upon reading the driest sort of nonsense from a prepared script. Congressional hearings are part solemn legislative session, part carnival, part high drama, and part transparent charade. In order to be truly effective, the presentation of your case before a congressional committee demands accuracy, forcefulness, and spontaneity.

If you have secured advance copies of other witnesses' written statements, do not make a public issue of that fact. You have gained an advantage by being able to take into account your opposition's as well as your allies' arguments when preparing your own testimony, but you should gloat only in private. If you do so publicly, you will not receive the same favor again.

Often, the committee will call panels of witnesses rather than individual witnesses. This is particularly the case when several witnesses share the same general perspective on the issue. However, unless specifically requested to do so by the committee chairman or staff, you should not volunteer to appear as a panel member in lieu of an individual appearance. The impact of your individual statement will be diluted if there are five other people at the witness table while you are testifying. Nevertheless, panels are such a common practice that you should expect to be on one. When this occurs, you can generally find out who will be sharing the table with you before the hearings begin—sometimes several days in advance. In this case, be sure to contact all of the other witnesses on your panel to coordinate testimony.

In most congressional hearings, witnesses are seated at a table facing a horseshoe-shaped dais. The members sit at the dais with the staffers behind them. Try to maintain eye contact throughout your statement, referring to your notes only briefly. You should be accompanied by at least one assistant who can arrange supplemental information and give it to you quickly if you are asked questions. You shouldn't have to fumble with papers when you are trying to be responsive.

Planting Questions

It may not seem proper that questions are actually planted with member of Congress before a congressional hearing, but if you are to be an effective Washington lobbyist, you will have to get over your queasiness and play the game by Washington rules. Few congressional staffs and even fewer members of Congress have the opportunity to fully research your issue before the hearing. They are unlikely to know the strong and weak points of your arguments or those of your opposition. Judicious questioning can bring these out.

Planting questions should not be considered a trick you play on your opponents. Answering leading questions can be one of the best ways for you to emphasize critical points, even when you have already discussed the issue in your primary testimony (known as your "testimony in chief"). Conversely, if a member of Congress can ask your opponent a direct question for which he or she is ill prepared, the results can be more devastating than a direct attack in your own testimony.

If you decide to plant questions, be sure to clear them with the staff of the committee as well as with the personal staff of the member posing the question. If your question appears fair and reasonable, the staffs will generally agree to have the member ask it. The most important thing about planting questions, however, is that you must also supply the answer to any query you plant. This is especially important for questions for your opposition. The member posing the question must be able to follow up his line of examination with a second or third query if the initial answer he receives is not satisfactory. He won't be able to do so unless he has been fully briefed. He must be given not only the answer you anticipate your opposition will give, but also factual information regarding your point of view. Planted questions can easily backfire unless your questioner is both adroit and knowledgeable.

Be sure the questions you plant that are to be directed to you are not softballs. A rhetorical question such as, "Isn't it true, Mr. Witness, that if your position is not adopted it will cost the taxpayer forty-five billion dollars for no appreciable benefit?" won't win you any points. Such questions are so transparently biased that your answer will convince no one. Your planted questions must preserve the semblance of neutrality even though you are obviously an advocate for a particular point of view. You cannot draw the member of Congress publicly too far onto your side of the issue if he or she is to maintain effectiveness as an arbiter.

Answering Questions

Answering questions in a congressional hearing is a finely developed art. Unlike in a courtroom trial, witnesses are not required or even expected to merely respond yes or no to questions. Unlike judges, members of Congress are not neutral adjudicators of fact. They are strongly biased and often exhibit their personal prejudices. This being the case, your answers to congressional questions should fit the circumstances—you should be as aggressive in answering questions as your questioner is in posing them.

Do not be intimidated by hostile questions. Politely but firmly insist that you be permitted to give complete answers to complex questions, and don't allow yourself to be bullied into answering yes or no to questions that have no simple response. If, for example, the president of the Flat Earth Society were asked whether his organization received any corporate contributions, he might answer, "Yes, approximately five percent of our total operating budget is provided by foundations that are in turn funded by corporations. We do not now nor have we ever accepted any direction or control from corporations." A mere affirmative answer to the question could leave the impression that the organization was somehow a toady to big business. Conversely, do not provide more information than the questions call for. For example, if you are asked, "Did you plant the story that appeared in this morning's *Washington Post* about this matter?" your answer should be succinct "No, we did not." This answer suffices even if you met with the *Post* reporter just the previous afternoon. No one "plants" stories in the *Washington Post*, as the *Post* itself will be glad to affirm.

In answering friendly questions, try to do so with a straight face even when they are obvious softballs. One trick is to make the question appear to be more complex than it really is. For instance, if the Flat Earth Society president were asked whether it was true that the Round Earth Amendments would cost the taxpayers $45 billion, he might respond that the $45 billion is a maximum estimate spread over a five-year period, but that the first-year costs would exceed $13 billion. In general, avoid demagoguery and attempt to make even your friendly questioner appear to be a model of propriety.

If more than one member of your group is sharing the witness table with you, it is sometimes a good idea to permit others to answer one or two of the questions, particularly if a query falls in their area of expertise. Often, a different perspective on a given question is useful; even different phraseology used by your associates may provide a useful insight.

If you are asked a question for which you have no ready answer or that will require additional research, say so immediately. Don't attempt to bluff. You are dealing with experts in the art, so don't attempt to con them. In the event that you cannot answer a question and offer to provide additional information at a later date, be sure to do so as soon as possible—preferably within forty-eight hours following the hearing so the issue is still fresh in their minds. The additional information should be supplied in writing to the committee staff, the committee chairman, the member who asked the question, and all other members of the committee who attended the hearing.

During the course of a hearing, other witnesses will also be asked questions, some of which you will wish you had been asked. If such questions are asked before you testify, don't be reluctant to answer them yourself in person—put them in your testimony in chief. If the questions occur after you testify, respond to them in writing (again within forty-eight hours) to the committee staff, the committee chairman, and all other members who attended the hearing.

In any follow-up answers, be sure to request that your response be included in the formal record.

Press Coverage

The press can be expected to cover relatively few congressional hearings. Every day there are literally scores of committee and subcommittee hearings on every imaginable issue. Your hearing, although it may seem phenomenally important to you, may be less than impressive to callous national editors of major newspapers. Difficult as this may be for you to accept, it is your obligation to make your issue newsworthy; you cannot merely blame the press for political myopia.

Every time you testify before a congressional committee, your organization should issue a press release. The release should summarize the testimony of your witness and should not exceed two pages. It should follow the press release form specified in chapter 5 and should be marked "Embargoed for Release Until [date and time of your testimony]." The press release should be distributed at least twelve hours before you are due to testify. If you wait until the actual testimony is given, you will often miss deadlines and get no coverage at all. You should also agree to make yourself available for questions by the press immediately following your testimony. Part of the value of testifying before a congressional committee is the coverage you will receive. You should maximize it.

The Record

During the congressional hearing, constant reference is made to the "record." Although this sounds extremely official, it is much less precise than you might imagine. In most congressional hearings, a professional stenographer transcribes the testimony of all witnesses. Don't take this too seriously. If you muff your testimony, you will have an opportunity to correct the record by judiciously editing those portions of the hearing transcript in which you spoke.

Before the hearing starts, be sure to speak with the stenographer and ask for a copy of the rough draft of the transcript as soon as it becomes available. You should also check with the secretary of the committee to make sure you will have an opportunity to correct your remarks. A week or so after the hearing, you will receive the draft transcript. Invariably, you will hardly recognize what you said. The stenographer will have included all the fumbles of your speech—all the "and, uh's," "you know's," and so on. Clean up the text and make changes as appropriate, and return your corrections to the committee. Be sure to keep a copy of the corrected transcript for yourself; it is not unknown for a transcript to be lost in the mail.

At the hearing you will pick up copies of the written statements of all other witnesses if you have not already done so. If your relations with the committee staff are good, you can also get unedited copies of the entire transcript including your opposition's statements. If the committee staff is less than cooperative, don't lose hope. The Hill still contracts for stenographic assistance, so you can sometimes get full transcripts from the reporting service that hired the stenographer. If you do go to the independent reporting service to get a complete copy of the transcript, be sure to inquire about the per-page cost. Some transcription services charge up to $1.45 a page for advance copies.

It is useful to have your written statement printed in the *Congressional Record* very shortly after the hearing, which can be done by following the guidelines in chapter 9. This assures wider readership of your position and is good public relations. As for the hearing record, after you get a corrected copy—which is usually published two to three months after the hearing—be sure to send it to all your supporters.

The congressional hearing is one of the best opportunities for you to lay out your public position with a maximum of media coverage. Although few hearings are as thoroughly covered as those seen on the network news, they are an indispensable part of the legislative process and should be exploited to your fullest advantage.

9

THE CONGRESSIONAL RECORD

"If they put Congress' collective brain in a grasshopper, it would hop backwards."

—Author unknown

What Is the *Congressional Record?*

If you believe the claims of some members of Congress, the *Congressional Record* is the repository of all political wisdom. It is cited as the authority for wildly varying claims and is footnoted in innumerable speeches, articles, books, and even learned journals. In reality, most of the information that appears in the *Congressional Record* can be cited only for the fact that it appears in the *Congressional Record*.

The *Record* is the minutes of legislative sessions, but it also includes hundreds of pages of partisan political speeches delivered by members, as well as other people's speeches, articles, charts, government studies, poetry, newspaper editorials, and recipes for cornbread. Members of Congress can insert material into the *Record* by placing it into the "hopper," a basket located on the secretary's or clerk's desk in the Senate or House chamber. Inserts are then collected by the secretary or clerk and passed on to the Government Printing Office. Until the late 20th century, it was impossible to distinguish between what a member of Congress had actually said on the floor of the Senate or the House and what he merely "tossed in the hopper." Now, if a member did not actually say the words that are printed, a discreet bullet precedes the printed version. The *Congressional Record* could never survive a truth-in-advertising investigation under the same standards applied to most commercial products.

Nevertheless, the *Record* is an indispensable tool for the lobbyist. The last dozen or so pages of the daily *Record* contain a relatively complete agenda of bills introduced, committee meetings scheduled, and votes recorded, along with an update on the cursory status of legislation. No lobbyist can do without the roll-call vote listings on important legislation. Sometimes even the debates are worth reading; certainly the members of Congress would like you to believe they are. They spend millions of dollars every year reprinting speeches that appeared in the *Record* and sending them to their constituents.

How to Be Included in the *Congressional Record*

Although the quality of debate in the *Congressional Record* may not meet nineteenth-century British parliamentary standards, it is still useful to have your views published there. In the first place, it's free. Second, reprints of a *Congressional Record* statement make impressive propaganda pieces for your supporters. Third, many Hill staffers read the *Record*, and you may as well reach this audience.

Getting your views reprinted in the *Record* will be one of your easiest tasks as a lobbyist. You need only prepare the documents to be inserted, check their accuracy, and give them to a member of Congress who is willing to toss them in the hopper. (You should deal principally with the member's staff when requesting his or her help in this matter.) *Congressional Record* insertions can include newspaper editorials favorable to your position, speeches given by proponents of your views, articles on your issue that have appeared in other publications, statements made before congressional hearings, and even specially prepared statements by the members of Congress themselves. You should always attempt to have the statements you have made before congressional hearings included in the *Record* (see chapter 8).

In preparing your insertions, draft a two-paragraph introduction that incorporates the member of Congress's approval of the documents to be inserted. You should also be extremely careful about the accuracy of these insertions. If comments placed in the *Record* are inaccurate or scandalous, the member may be somewhat embarrassed, but your reputation will be severely damaged. The marginal gains achieved by having information printed in the *Record* are outweighed by the harm erroneous material can cause.

Reprinting of Remarks

After a member of Congress has placed an item in the *Congressional Record*, he or she will often have that portion of the publication reprinted as a one- or two-page flier for distribution to constituents. Congressional reprints can be used for general information purposes, as campaign propaganda, in research, and for other nonlegislative activities.

Each congressional office has its own method of handling the enormous cost of reprinting and distributing items from the *Record*. If the member chooses to reprint an item related to your cause, you may able to help him and your group by absorbing part of the expense of mailing it to your own members. You should, however, be extremely sensitive to the legal and political implications of any suggestion that you provided financial assistance. If necessary, the member of Congress's staff can request a ruling from the Ethics Committee regarding this issue.

If you cannot convince the member to distribute the reprinted *Record* item at his or her own expense, you may still be able to get additional copies for your group at very low cost. Consult with the congressional office about using government printing services for this purpose.

10

THE STAFF

"A politician is a person with whose politics you don't agree; if you agree with him, he is a statesman."

—David Lloyd George

Who Are They? What Motivates Them?

At last count, congressional staff members numbered over twenty thousand—not counting the five thousand or so in support positions such as police officers, doormen, etc. Staffers are the backbone of the Hill. No legislation is passed or defeated without their agreement or at least acquiescence. They are, in effect, the fourth branch of government. Given their enormous power, they obviously play an important role in any lobbying campaign.

As often as not, staff members are ignored by inexperienced lobbyists—who, as often as not, lose. Many such lobbyists believe that if they deliver their message to a congressman or senator personally, nothing else matters; this assumption is almost always false. If a lobbyist ignores the staff, a meeting with a member of Congress will be for the sake of appearances only. The member will generally exude sympathy for the lobbyist's cause and mutter vague promises about future action. The moment the lobbyist leaves the room, the member will call in a staffer and demand to know what the prior conversation was all about. If the staff member has not been thoroughly briefed by the lobbyist, he or she will almost certainly scuttle any request the lobbyist has made to the boss.

It is an anomaly of American politics that a vast majority of Hill staffers are under thirty years old. Phenomenal power has been given to people who have little experience in the real world. Many lobbyists tend to regard dealing with these young staff members as a distasteful necessity. The staff members react accordingly. They know they are inexperienced in many of the areas in which they must work, but they deeply resent condescension. Overworked, harassed, and often ignored, they still know that they are an essential part of the legislative process. These are intelligent, sensitive people. Although hardened by politics and generally immune to outright flattery, they want respect. A good lobbyist will give it to them.

Keep in mind that congressional staffs are influenced by a variety of job demands:

Protecting the Member

Staff members' first obligation is to protect their boss. They will be extremely cautious about advising the member to take positions that could stir controversy and expose him or her to criticism. They will also make sure that the member is well briefed before stating a position so he or she doesn't end up looking like a fool in public.

Promoting the Member

One of the primary roles of staffers is to get their boss reelected. Their jobs depend upon it. Constituent problems are thus a top priority for most congressional offices. Staffers spend almost 80 percent of their time on constituent services, hoping to convince the voters that the member—and they—should keep their jobs. If you can convince the staff that your position will improve the member's chance at reelection, you are already halfway home.

Researching and Briefing

Every year, over ten thousand separate bills are introduced in the Congress; that's over a million pages of proposed legislation. Members of Congress cannot hope to read all these bills themselves, so they rely on their staffs to brief them on the fine points of the potential laws. However, even staffers get overwhelmed by the deluge of paper. They can call upon the Congressional Research Service to prepare briefing papers, but these papers are almost always neutral. They state facts, not political reasons.

As a lobbyist, your job is to do the staffers' work for them. Staff members will be uniformly grateful if you provide them with short, straightforward, accurate, and honest briefing papers.

Structure of the Congressional Staff System

The congressional staff system is as complex as any military organization. In general, however, it can be broken down into two separate parts: the personal staff and the issue or committee staff. The personal staff of a congressman or senator will generally be organized into the hierarchical structure shown below.

Personal Staff of a Congressman or Senator

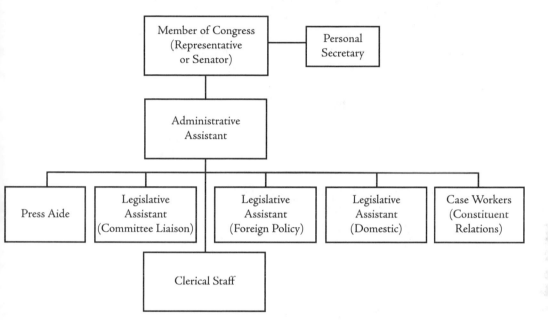

The precise titles of staff members will vary from office to office. "Personal assistant" is sometimes used instead of "personal secretary." "Professional staff" or "legislative director" is often a replacement for "legislative assistant," and "chief of staff" is sometimes substituted for "administrative assistant." Whatever the titles, the roles of various staff members will usually follow the same scheme.

The Administrative Assistant

An administrative assistant (AA), particularly on the House side, is almost always the most powerful person on the staff. The AA's role is not only to run the day-to-day operations of the congressional office, but also to screen all issues on which the member must make decisions. AAs prioritize whom the member of Congress must see, which speeches he or she must give, and what constituents require attention. (In the Senate, where staffs are organizationally more complex, this screening function might be performed by a senior legislative assistant, leaving the AA to strictly administrative duties.) A good AA must have Machiavellian political instincts, as well as organizational ability, patience, charm, and on occasion, a nasty temper.

Administrative assistants are rarely issue oriented. They have neither the time nor the inclination to learn the minutiae of legislative proposals. Their job is to reduce the hundreds of demands upon a congressman or senator to a manageable number and to present the member with clear-cut options for each issue they feel is worthy of the member's attention. Even in poorly run offices, it is difficult to present an issue effectively to the member if the AA has not already decided it is a matter about which the member should be concerned.

Almost without exception, administrative assistants are more impressed by political reality than by the merits of a lobbyist's position. Therefore, when explaining the facts of your case to an administrative assistant, always emphasize the politics of the member's state or district. An AA will be as concerned about the number of constituents who will be directly affected by your legislative proposals as about the details of your position. As noted above, the most important goal in almost any congressional office is reelection. Members seek to avoid taking any action that would antagonize a significant bloc of voters. Conversely, the promise of more votes is as important to most members as a pledge of financial support. If your group has votes, it has power—even if it lacks a thick wallet. You need to communicate that fact to the AA.

Your position's economic impact upon a member's state or district is also an important factor to emphasize when speaking with an administrative assistant. Even if very few constituents might be directly affected, the moneymaking potential within the state or district should not be overlooked. Successful lobbyists will also try to emphasize the emotional impact of their proposal on the member's constituents. Even if the issue is not financially vital to the voters, it may be politically charged. For example, particularly on the West Coast, environmental issues have a high visibility factor that is not necessarily related to the monetary costs or benefits to the constituencies. In these areas, environmentalists are extremely well organized and often tend to be one-issue voters.

Other things that would attract an administrative assistant to your position are the following:

◆Suggest that the member's support would be widely publicized in your organization's newsletter and e-mail bulletins and on your Web page. This is free publicity for the member. Since your group is sponsoring it, the publicity is almost guaranteed to be positive. Further, it effectively represents free political propaganda, which few members of Congress are apt to refuse.

♦Suggest that your organization could issue press releases welcoming the member's support. Such a release costs little and is more likely to be picked up by the press than a statement from the member's own office.

♦Suggest to the administrative assistant that the member be invited to a well-publicized function in his or her state or district where your supporters would commend him or her. Congressmen and senators love these events, especially when they can be turned into photo opportunities. There are many other types of staged events that can serve as photo opportunities. An environmentalist group might stage a walk-through of an area they wish to have preserved as wilderness. Unions, companies, and businessmen might invite the member to their plants to speak directly to the workers. Railroads might invite members of Congress to sit in locomotive cabs. Angry neighbors of airports might present the member with earmuffs while standing at the end of a busy runway. The possibilities are endless, but be sure to invite the press and emphasize the photo opportunity. You might also want to have one or two of your own photographers present to add an air of importance to the affair.

When trying to impress an administrative assistant, a temperate approach is usually the most successful. Of all the people on Capitol Hill, administrative assistants are least influenced by cheerleaders or harbingers of doom. It is almost never appropriate to threaten members of Congress in front of their AAs, even indirectly. The administrative assistants—the alter egos of the members—will react similarly to the way the members themselves would.

If an administrative assistant generally agrees with your approach, suggest to him or her that the details be worked out at the staff level and in consultation with the congressman or senator. You should also brief the legislative assistant assigned to the project. If any press releases or publicity stunts are to be included as a price for the member's support, be sure to include the member's press aide in your future discussions.

Depending upon the office, the administrative assistant may be the most important person you see. Some AAs literally control their bosses. In other offices, the AAs have somewhat less power. But there are no offices in which you can afford to ignore them.

The Personal Secretary

Notwithstanding all the stories of congressional secretaries who can't dial a telephone (much less type), most Hill secretaries are competent, loyal, and dedicated. The personal secretary is the staffer who works most closely with the member. She (I say *she* because almost all personal secretaries in the House and Senate are women, the Congress being exempt from equal employment opportunity requirements by law) will be the one who arranges the member's day card. These day cards are carried by virtually every member and were historically three-by-five-inch index cards containing the member's schedule for the day. Increasingly, day cards are now electronic calendars maintained and updated on PDAs.

Although the personal secretary can sometimes be countermanded by the administrative assistant or the member, she is generally the one who actually keeps the member's schedule. As such, she may suggest which persons or groups the member should see, in which events the member will participate, and even when the member will take a vacation. She also actually receives the member's telephone calls and must decide on the spot which callers are important enough to put through—and which will be routed through Alexandria, Egypt, and swallowed by the telephone system in Dundalk, New York.

Although personal secretaries are not charged with making policy decisions on specific political issues, they are the master sergeants of Capitol Hill—nothing can be accomplished without them. You may not need their support, but you cannot afford their enmity. Make it a point to get to know the personal secretaries of all the members of Congress with whom you have regular dealings. Not only will they help you in relations with the member, but they will also be an invaluable source of information on the member's preferences. They also know quite a bit about other offices on the Hill, and as you get to know them better, they can be a prime source of gossip as well as hard facts.

Personal secretaries can be extremely useful to a lobbyist in helping to arrange functions on the Hill. As a private citizen, you have no direct access to Hill facilities such the three dozen Hill committee rooms or special party rooms. These can, however, be provided if requested by a member of Congress (whose account will be charged). If you would like to have a function in one of them, a member's private secretary can arrange it for you. In addition, she can prove invaluable by running interference for you with the catering bureaucracy on the Hill and by making sure that the members of Congress you invited to your function will actually show up.

Few people pay personal secretaries the respect they feel they deserve. For example, although many secretaries prefer to be called by their first names, there are some who deeply resent it. Be sensitive to this and follow the lead of the staff. If they refer to her as "Ms. Brown," do so yourself until you get to know her better.

The Press Aide

In most congressional offices, the press aide is not at all what you would expect. Usually, press aides have no particular qualifications for their jobs other than having worked on the member's campaign staff. In the offices of junior members, the press aide often serves two or three other functions—usually including that of a legislative assistant. But the aide's main function is to write press releases about what a wonderful job the member is doing for his or her district or state. These releases, of course, are delivered to the media, and they are almost always posted on the member's Web site.

Press aides are overworked, underloved, and subject to unreasonable deadlines. This gives you a significant advantage in dealing with them. If you give them a statement for the member, they are often delighted to reprint it virtually word for word. They may tinker with a few of the phrases, but generally they will leave your piece untouched.

In preparing a press release for a member of Congress, the primary rule is to make sure it is individualized for that office. A release prepared for one member should never be given to any other congressional office in the same form. Releases are personalized by relating them to a member's state or district or committee activities. You can also insert a tactful reference to your group.

The press release should be printed in a standard format on plain bond paper—not your letterhead—or submitted on disk or as an e-mail attachment. This will enable the press aide to claim credit for preparing the release, but you will not have deceived the congressional office as to the origin of the document. This is important. If you feel that either the press aide or the aide's office would regard this procedure as deceptive, be more straightforward.

A sample press release is as follows:

For Immediate Release

Congressman Bigelow Labels Round
Earth Bill a Taxpayer Rip-Off

Washington, [date]. Congressman James T. Bigelow (D-Pa.) today labeled the Round Earth Amendments Bill "a taxpayer rip-off that would do nothing to promote science but would feed an already bloated federal bureaucracy." Speaking before the Flat Earth Society National Convention, the congressman said, "Certain people in this country want to get the government in the business of promoting their own ideology at taxpayer expense. I, for one, want no part of that." The congressman went on to say that he had consistently supported prudence in federal spending and saw government support for Round Earth theory as yet another example of government waste. "Public funds are a public trust," said Bigelow. "They should not be used for any special interest group's purposes." The congressman warned the delegates that the Round Earth Bill had considerable support in the Congress, and pledging his continued opposition to this legislation, concluded, "If passage of this ill-conceived measure appears inevitable, I will do my best to assure that equivalent funds are appropriated to present the other point of view." The Round Earth Amendments Bill would provide federal funds for instruction in Round Earth theory at the elementary and junior high school levels. For further information contact: Rob Greenspan, Media Relations Director for Cong. Bigelow, (202) 555-0142.

The above example may appear a monument to hypocrisy, but it is only a slightly altered version of an actual release from a congressional office. (Names, of course, have been changed to protect the innocent.) It is not even an outrageous example. Most congressional press releases are more cleverly written, but all have a singular purpose: to promote particular issues and ultimately to promote the members themselves.

The press aide also edits the member's so-called newsletter to constituents—a thinly disguised propaganda piece designed to inform the electorate on the member's activities in Washington. It is usually a four-to-eight-page pamphlet covering half a dozen issues, and it will often have pictures of the member meeting with various groups. An extremely effective way to promote your cause is to have a feature article on it included in a member's newsletter. It's free, it reaches over fifty thousand people by first-class mail, and it's the closest thing to a free lunch you'll find in Washington.

Press aides are also impressed if you can put them in touch with sympathetic reporters. Strange as it may seem, most congressmen and senators have a difficult time getting their names in print on a regular basis. This is one of the press aide's main responsibilities, and it is usually easier to get him or her to agree to a meeting with a reporter than with a lobbying group. After all, reporters need only call the congressional office if they want a story, but they often do not return phone calls from junior members of Congress. You should use such meetings to get press coverage for your issue. A meeting will always be most effective if you have thoroughly briefed the press aide beforehand. An earnest statement expressing the member's support of your position can be very persuasive to a reporter, particularly if it is accompanied by a press release from the member's office.

If a member's support for your position is wavering, and you have a strong membership presence in the member's state or district, it is sometimes better if you contact the local media *before* contacting the member's press aide. Brief the reporter on your issue and express some doubt about the member's position. The reporter, if urged, will call the press aide. Given the Watergate mentality of most Washington reporters, they can usually intimidate a press aide into committing the congressman or senator to a particular position. If you have played your cards carefully and honestly—the press aide (who is often cited as a "reliable source" in news stories) will commit the member to supporting your position in public. Even if the aide equivocates, your issue will be brought to the member's attention. Of course, it is better to work with the press aide than to resort to backdoor methods—but, then, if a member has already agreed to support you there is no need for such tricks.

The news media can be a powerful tool when used to your advantage. Once the media gets involved, congressional offices would rather support than oppose you. But be very judicious in siccing a reporter on a congressional office. It is likely to backfire unless you have carefully briefed the press aide.

Press aides, if played correctly, can be the most easily manipulated of all congressional staffers. They have inordinate demands placed upon them and are, in Tom Wolfe's parlance, the "flak catchers" of Capitol Hill. Anything you do to make their lives easier will be rewarded.

The Legislative Assistant

Legislative assistants (LAs) are the people with whom you should have the greatest contact on the Hill. They are the experts on specific legislative issues. Their views will be translated into speeches for the member of Congress. Their opinions will usually determine the member's views on your subject. In short, they can make you or break you. Nothing can be more useful to a lobbyist than the sympathetic ear of a legislative assistant. Even if an LA is not as fully briefed on the matter as you are, his or her trust is the most important commodity you can have.

It is the LA to whom you will explain your issue and who will rely on you for additional information. With an LA, as opposed to an AA, you can concentrate less on politics and more on facts. If the member's office is sympathetic to your position, do not be afraid to lay out all the facts—favorable and unfavorable—and work out an action plan with him or her. Together, the two of you should distill the issue into a politically defensible position.

During all your discussions, you should maintain one image: that of a provider. Although the LA has sources you cannot hope to duplicate (such as the Congressional Research Service), you should offer to undertake any research, grassroots action, press contact, or other effort that would promote your position. Unless the LA volunteers for a project, do not suggest that he or she perform any administrative or research function.

Legislative assistants can often intercede for you with administrative assistants and the members themselves. If you have been successful in convincing them of the rectitude of your cause, they can even overcome opposition from above. LAs are essential to you. Forget them at your peril.

The Committee Staffs

Most Hill staffers do not work for members' personal staffs, but in the three dozen committees of the House and Senate. Some committee staffs employ upward of sixty people, and most have at least twenty-five professional and clerical employees. Although Hill committee staff members are supposed to merely provide support for the committee members, their jobs are intensely political. The partisan makeup of the committee will dictate the number of majority and minority staff members it has. In most cases, senior committee staff members are appointed by the ranking senator or congressman of each party serving on that committee. They are thus an adjunct to that congressman or senator's personal staff and represent one of the fringe benefits of seniority.

This seniority rule is not immutable. It is therefore useful to find out in advance which senator or congressman sponsored the appointment of the committee staff member with whom you will be dealing. Judicious use of the sponsor's name during your dealings with the staff member can be extremely useful.

As with the personal staffs of congressmen and senators, your relations with committee staffs should be characterized by openness and honesty. You should, however, expect to be much more technical with the committee staffs than you were with an individual member's personal staff. Each congressional committee staff will have several lawyers on the payroll, but even the nonlegal staff members tend to think in legalistic terms. You are now dealing with the experts on the intent, substance, and implementation of legislation; in many cases you will be speaking with people who actually wrote the existing legislation in the field. The vague language you might have used with a member's AA or LA will not suffice.

Committee staffers will be interested in your specific proposals and the precise language you would like to implement or defeat, and they will judge your position more on its merits than anyone else you speak to on the Hill. They will be the most critical of your statistics and will have no difficulty checking your figures. But they can also be your greatest ally in getting your issue appropriately addressed. A committee staff member who believes your position has merit will rarely encounter a technical argument from a congressman or senator's personal staff.

You should prepare yourself for a meeting with a committee staff member by reading and rereading the existing law, the proposed changes, and any backup material you can find—you need to know more about the subject than the staffer does. Since committee staff members spend their entire lives considering the subject matter in which you are interested, this might seem to be a monumental task. But don't be intimidated—the staff members probably will not have focused on the technical aspects of your particular piece of legislation. There are only three dozen committees to handle more than a million pages of proposed legislation, so staffers simply do not have the time to work out the details that you can provide.

You will also want to meet with staff counsel, the person who actually writes the laws being considered by the committee. With the authorization of a congressional office, he or she can assist you in preparing actual legislative language. Even if you think you have done an adequate job in drafting proposed legislation, or are actively opposing legislation written by someone else, it is still a good idea to spend some time with legislative counsel. Although they are among the most important people on Capitol Hill, they are ignored by most lobbyists. They sincerely appreciate any attention they receive and your time with them will be well spent.

The Initial Contact

Your initial contact with a member of Congress's personal staff will often be through a routine call to the member's office. Simply inquire which person in the office is in charge of your issue. Even if the person answering the phone has never heard of you or your issue, he or she will connect you to someone who has. In most congressional offices, the majority of the personal staff are devoted to constituent matters (e.g., finding lost Social Security checks, arranging admissions to military academies, answering routine mail, etc.). Many of the staffers are fairly junior and don't have a lot to do with actual legislation. About the only people to see on most legislative matters are the LAs (or the AA). The balance of the staff are often irrelevant for lobbying purposes.

When you approach committee staff members, it is desirable to first isolate the individual responsible for the legislation in subcommittee. Call the subcommittee office and ask the first person to whom you speak which staff member is responsible for your issue. Invariably the first information you receive will be incorrect. You should, however, call the person to whom you are referred; he or she will refer you to someone else. After two or three telephone calls you should finally arrive at the right desk. One trick in this procedure is to have a legal pad in front of you when making these calls. Write down every name and number you are given so you can say who referred you to whom. In any event, you may need to go back to someone else on the list in the future. When you find the appropriate committee staff member, give him or her a brief outline of the issue you would like to discuss and arrange for a personal meeting. Be sure you have the contact's correct telephone number and e-mail address. As soon as you hang up the phone, check out the person with whom you spoke in one of the sources listed in chapter 19.

Remember, each committee staff member generally has a counterpart staffer from the other political party. Of course, since the majority party will have more staffers, it can subdivide issues more finely. For example, a majority staff may have a person in charge of issue A and another whose responsibility is issue B, while both issues are handled by a single staffer on the minority side of the aisle. You will want to speak with that person at some point as well, if only to keep him or her informed about what you are doing, but be very sensitive in this matter. Going to the minority party can sometimes be helpful if the ranking majority member on the subcommittee is either not interested in or is opposed to your position, but minority members rarely have the power of a majority party subcommittee member.

A note about e-mails to staff: there is no public e-mail directory for Hill staffers. Even when they are available, staff e-mail address books are notoriously out of date. Staffers often guard their real contact information to avoid being swamped with messages. They will, however, reveal their e-mail address if you ask them directly—and if you give them a good reason to do so.

Lunch?

A lunch meeting is a traditional way to introduce yourself to staff in Washington, but be *very* careful with this ploy. Given the current scrutiny over congressional ethics, lunch dates are a sensitive issue in most offices. New ethics rules strictly forbid staffers from accepting meals from lobbyists except in very limited circumstances; they must pay for themselves at any lunch meeting. Thus, it is wise not to invite a staffer to a fancy restaurant. It is not unusual for lunch tabs in Washington to run to over forty dollars per person, staffers don't ordinarily make a lot of money, and they can be seriously burned financially if they have to pony up that kind of cash or risk violating an ethics rule. Opt instead for the cafeterias in the House and Senate office buildings (there are several). Try to arrive a little early for lunch.

While at lunch, give the staff member only a very general outline of your position and try to find out how much he or she knows about the issue under consideration. You do not want to condescend to a person who already knows more than you do about the subject, nor do you want to overwhelm someone who has never heard of your issue before. Feel the staffer out on a subject related to your own; try to develop a personal rapport.

After lunch, decide whether it would be advantageous to go back to the staffer's office. Be extremely sensitive to his or her schedule. Some staffers don't have the luxury of an extended lunch. You may also find appointments canceled or curtailed because of changes in the legislative schedule. In short, don't be pushy. If you do have the opportunity to accompany the staffer back to the office, you should be ready to lay out your whole case in less than fifteen minutes. By this time, you should have determined how much the staffer knows about your subject and the best areas to explore in the future.

Almost invariably, you will find that there are several issues on which staff members are not fully briefed. Be sure to take careful notes on these points. (Many lobbyists do this on a legal pad. Although it's bulky, you can put a lot of information on it and it looks official.) On every issue for which the staffer requests additional information, be sure to respond very promptly, usually within twenty-four hours. You should also make it a habit to get back in touch with the staff member on at least a weekly basis, preferably every third or fourth day. Remember, you're going to be discussing the technical aspects of your issue with this person; this can't be accomplished in one day.

11

THE CONGRESSIONAL VISIT

"In order to become the master, the politician poses as the servant."

—Charles de Gaulle

The tradition most associated with Washington lobbying is the actual pressing of the flesh with a congressman or senator. Although few congressional lobbying campaigns ignore this tradition, seldom has success resulted from a concentration on face-to-face meetings to the exclusion of other lobbying methods, particularly good staff contacts and adequate homework.

Meeting a member of Congress may be only a small part of a complete lobbying program, but it is essential nevertheless, and you should be sure to include it in your plans.

Whom to See

Most of the real work of a lobbying campaign is done at the staff level and through your letter-writing and grassroots campaigns. It is essential, however, that you be in direct personal contact with your congressional allies. You should also plan on seeing swing members, whether they agree with your position or not. (A swing member is one who can either control a number of other votes or decide a particular issue with his or her own vote. This includes committee and subcommittee chairmen, ranking minority members of all appropriate committees and subcommittees, and any other members of Congress who are known to have an active interest in your position.) Finally, you owe a visit to members of Congress whose constituencies are particularly favorable to your position.

Before meeting with anyone, you should prepare a list of all members of Congress with whom you wish to speak. In most cases, you can develop a must-see list and a secondary list of members whom it would be helpful but not essential to have on your side.

When visiting a member of Congress who is not directly involved with your issue in committee, you should go out of your way to be sure that he or she is aware of a vital constituent interest in your matter. It is best if you can include one of the member's constituents in the group that meets with him or her—but never permit a powerful but uninformed constituent to speak for your group, even in the confines of a member's office. The constituent in question should always be accompanied by a person who is adequately briefed on all the issues and who is capable of following up on any questions that may arise during the course of the meeting.

The Summary Sheet

For each of the congressmen and senators on your list, you should prepare a summary sheet. This will include data on the member; almost all of this information is available from public sources, but the emphasis here will be on your particular issue.

The summary sheet should include analyses of what other groups think about the member. Dozens of lobbying organizations rank members according to how they vote on issues of concern to those organizations. The weight given to each vote and each issue varies from group to group, so the rankings compiled by one organization may not be directly comparable to another's grading policies. You should carefully note precisely what criteria are used by each group before making any sweeping judgments. Despite this caveat, a review of such rankings can provide a general idea of the political proclivities of a member and is a useful tool for preliminary analysis.

A sample summary sheet might be as follows:

Congresswoman Sybil Simpatico (D-N.M.)
Second District

Biography
Born: March 12, 1936, Belmont, N.J.; Home: Lovington, N.M.; B.S.: Harvard, 1951; J.D.: Yale, 1954; Married, three children; Catholic; Career: Securities Exchange commission, 1955–56; Nasty, Poor, Brutish, and Short (law firm), Santa Fe, 1956–62 (partner, 1960); N.M. Senate, 1961–64; elected U.S. House of Representatives, 1964; Committees: Interior and Insular Affairs; Subcommittees: Mine and Mining, Oversight/Special Investigations, Water and Power Resources.

Ratings

ADA	COPE	ACA	NTU	NAB	NSI*
20	34	63	50	46	60

Key Votes on Flat Earth Issues

Special Department of Education Appropriations	For
National Science Foundation Special Grants	Against
NASA Propaganda	For
Local School Control	For
HEW Appropriations	For

Constituent Contacts

♦Alistair Greely: Albuquerque Flat Earth Society, Local 4 (fifty members); thirty confirmed letters to members of Congress (February–March)

♦Jennifer Bell: major contributor, Las Cruces, N.M.; member, Flat Earth Society, Local 14

♦Janet Wilenska: chairman, Flat Earth Caucus; N.M. Democratic Party; member, Flat Earth Society, Local 31

Staff

John Border (LA/Constituent Services): (555-0125)
Carol Matheson (Secretary to Mr. Border)

---

*Organizations providing ratings include:

ADA: Americans for Democratic Action, 1625 K Street NW, Suite 210, Washington, DC 20006. This is generally regarded as the premier liberal political organization in the United States, and its ratings reflect explicitly liberal values.

COPE: AFL-CIO Committee on Political Education, 815 16th Street NW, Washington, DC 20006. This rating reflects the point of view of the nation's largest organized labor organization.

PC: Public Citizen, 1600 20th Street NW, Washington, DC 20009 and 215 Pennsylvania Avenue SE, Washington, DC 20003. This is an organization founded by Ralph Nader in 1971; it tends to reflect his views.

RIPON: The Ripon Society, 1300 L Street NW, Washington, DC 20005. This is a group of people who identify themselves as liberal Republicans.

NFU: National Farmers Union, 400 Capitol Street NW, Suite 790, Washington, DC 20001. This farmers' organization tends to be closer in views to Democrats than Republicans, in contrast to, among others, the American Farm Bureau Federation, which does not issue ratings.

NTU: National Taxpayers Union, 108 North Alfred Street, Alexandria, VA 22314. This group wants to cut government spending and compiles a rating based on every spending vote in the Congress during the year.

CFA: Consumers Federation of America, 1620 I Street NW, Suite 200, Washington, DC 20006. This group describes itself as pro-consumer.

NSI: National Security Index of the American Security Council, 101 Constitution Avenue NW, Suite 800, Washington, DC 20001. This index reflects support for major defense expenditures and military programs.

The next page of the summary sheet should outline your presentation to this particular member of Congress, stressing the factors you wish to discuss with him or her. You should tailor the summary sheet to the particular issues that will affect the member's vote, with particular emphasis on constituent relationships and local issues.

Arranging a Visit

After you have prepared your summary sheet and contacted your constituent members, you should arrange for a meeting with the member of Congress by telephoning his or her personal secretary. You can get in touch with the secretary either directly or through one of your staff contacts. Tell the staffer with whom you speak that you will take no more than fifteen minutes of the member's time, and emphasize the proposed presence of the member's constituent at the meeting. If possible, the meeting should be arranged for a time when the member's committee is not scheduled for a session, and when the staffer can clear his or her own calendar—for reasons that we will examine in the next section, you will want to include the staffer in the meeting with the boss. After you have arranged a time, be sure to coordinate with your own members who will be attending the meeting.

All these arrangements should be made at least a week prior to the actual appointment. Be sure to fax or e-mail the senator or congressman's personal secretary a brief summary of the issue you will be discussing and the names and positions of the persons who will be accompanying you to the meeting.

Staff Contact

For practical as well as political reasons, you must be sure that the persons with whom you have been dealing on the congressional staff are fully briefed on the reasons for the meeting. It should not appear that you are attempting to go over the staff members' heads in meeting with their boss, merely that you have a constituent with a personal message for the member. You must handle the situation with extreme diplomacy. Remember, the staffers will be advising the member on your issue. You cannot afford to alienate them at any stage, and a sure way to do so is to embarrass them in front of their superior.

Before the meeting, the staffers will have already briefed the boss. When you arrive at the office, the member will have a very good idea of the issues you wish to raise, as well as a proposed plan of action. You should work with the staffers on briefing papers that they will give to the member. In some offices, the staff will want to have dossiers on the constituent you will be bringing, on you, and on your group. You should provide these upon request.

Failure to brief the relevant staff members is not merely a breach of protocol; it can be destructive to your entire presentation. As mentioned earlier, if once the meeting is over and you have left the room, the member of Congress turns to a staff aide and says, "What the hell was that all about?" and the aide doesn't know, you might just as well have stayed home.

What to Say and How to Say It

Your meeting is arranged; you have briefed the staff, prepared your summary sheets, and made sure your constituent is aware of the issues. Now you must explain your position to the actual member of Congress.

Be sure to arrive at the member's office about five minutes early. Although you may have a specific appointment time, Hill schedules are infuriatingly flexible. Congressmen and senators are called for record votes, committee meetings, constituent hand-holding, and a dozen other distractions. You cannot afford to have your own tardiness derail your meeting. On the other hand, to maintain a good reputation with members of your own group, you cannot afford to keep them waiting in a member's anteroom for longer than fifteen to twenty minutes. Be sure to tell everyone in your group to turn off his or her cell phone. It is astonishing how many carefully arranged meetings have been wrecked by inopportune ring tones.

When you arrive, first ask to see the members of the staff who will be sitting in on the meeting. You should discuss any last-minute developments with them and introduce them to the other people in your delegation. Eventually you will be ushered into the boss's office. If you have not met this congressman or senator before, the staffers should be given the opportunity to introduce you. If you have met, take the initiative and say how glad you are to see him or her again—stressing the *again*—and introduce your other delegation members. Next, tell the congressman or senator how much you have appreciated the staffers' assistance (the staff members, of course, will smile modestly). Be sure to do this even if the staff members have been sitting on their hands for the past six weeks. You're not necessarily giving thanks for past assistance; praise is fertilizer for future relationships.

Give the member a one-page write-up of your issue and your position. (Be sure *not* to give the member the summary sheet concerning his background described earlier in this chapter.) If the staffers have done their jobs, the member will already have been briefed on most of the salient points, but you should stress the elements outlined in your write-up. If you have a constituent attending the meeting, that person should do most of the introductory presentation; you should merely fill in as necessary. If no constituent is present, you should still highlight the ways in which your case will benefit the member's constituents.

During the course of the meeting, take careful notes on both the points made and the questions asked of you—keep a legal pad on your lap for that purpose. Do not take notes on a laptop. Although it may seem more efficient, tapping on a keyboard during meetings with a member is distracting and vaguely disrespectful. The practice is slowly gaining acceptance, but err on the side of caution unless a staffer is taking in this manner. Invariably, a staff member will be keeping notes in some format; you will want to compare them to your own after the meeting.

Never under any circumstances should you attempt to intimidate, threaten, or bribe the member or make promises that you cannot keep. Most members of Congress simply will not respond to threats, bribes, unsupported allegations, or skullduggery. That does not mean your presentation should be formal, however. You and your constituent should be straightforward, frank, and explicit. You should present your case and ask the member in specific terms to commit to your objectives. This is a briefing session, but more important, you are attempting to get him or her to commit to a favorable or at least neutral position on your issue. Remind the member of his or her past votes and the issues involved in them. Stress the factual and political factors that you feel are most important to him or her, taking your lead from the staff members present. If someone in your delegation gets out of line, cut that person off short; you cannot afford the enmity of a congressman or senator for personal reasons. Above all, keep your comments short. You should be able to present your entire case in fifteen minutes unless the member extends the meeting by asking questions.

Be polite; be succinct; be aggressive. Don't be awed by a member's title. Since you have only fifteen minutes, you should not be distracted by secondary issues—stick to the subject. Politicians have a penchant for diverting the conversation from uncomfortable subjects; don't let that happen to you.

At the conclusion of the meeting, leave a typed list of the names, titles, and addresses of all your people who attended the meeting so that the member can assess your importance and write follow-up letters if appropriate. You should also leave business cards. Often, the other members of your delegation will not have formal cards, but no matter how cursory your lobbying effort, you should have them made for yourself. They should be distributed not only at congressional meetings, but also at any session you have with staff members. A business card need not be elaborate. Your name, organization, address, e-mail address, and telephone number on a simple white card is sufficient. These cards can be printed at minimal cost in Washington and are de rigueur for any remotely serious lobbyist. Even if you have ample funds, multicolored or unique cards may not justify the expense. If you wish to be more elaborate, a heavy, engraved card is preferable to a flashy fold-out.

Follow-Up

After the meeting, you and all the other participants in your group should write thank-you letters to the member. All participants should also write separate thank-you letters, or at least e-mail messages, to the staff members who took part. If you have been dealing with a particular staff member who was not able to attend the meeting, you should send that person a letter informing him or her of the meeting and the relative success you achieved.

In your thank-you letters, be sure to restate the basic points you made during the meeting itself and ask the member of Congress to take action on your behalf. A sample letter might read as follows:

The Honorable Sybil Simpatico
United States House of Representatives
Washington, DC 20515

Dear Congresswoman Simpatico:

On behalf of myself and the entire Flat Earth Society, I want to thank you again for your courtesy in seeing us on September 23. All of us, and in particular Jennifer Bell, express our deepest appreciation for your courtesy. We were especially encouraged by your expression of support for Flat Earthism and opposition to the Round Earth Bill.

This, in our view, is an extremely serious matter and is likely to result in a very close vote on the House floor in the near future. The Round Earth Amendments are not only an ill-disguised attempt by federal bureaucrats to dictate the scientific theology of local school districts but also a consummate waste of taxpayers' funds. Further, as you are aware, a majority of voters in your district steadfastly oppose the philosophy inherent in Round Earthism. We hope we can count on you to use whatever influence you have to defeat this bill in committee; failing that, it can be beaten on the floor. As you requested, I have enclosed additional information regarding the impact of Round Earthism on the Department of Education's appropriations for next year. If you need any additional data, please do not hesitate to contact me.

Sincerely,
Linda Borcum
Flat Earth Society

cc: John Border

About a week after your meeting, you should call the member's staff to make sure the member has performed the tasks he or she promised. This should be done in a very low-key manner; no one likes to be nagged, but nag you must if you are to be successful. As soon as the congressman or senator acts on a promise, you should be sure to write even more effusive thank-you letters and tell your constituents that the member has kept his or her word.

12

ALLIES

"A Sympathizer would seem to imply a certain degree of benevolent feeling. Nothing of the kind. It signifies a ready-made accomplice in any species of political villainy."

—Thomas Love Peacock

As noted in chapter 3, identifying your friends and opponents should be one of your first objectives in a lobbying campaign. It is, however, only half the job. You must turn this knowledge to your advantage. Although you will not be dealing closely with your enemies, you should have a good working relationship with your allies. This chapter focuses primarily on how to treat your friends, both on the Hill and elsewhere.

Government Agencies

Your most valuable allies in any congressional matter may not be in the Congress at all. Virtually all legislation affects some government department, bureau, agency, or commission, and almost without exception, these administrative bodies dearly love to see the scope of their authority expanded. The agency that is charged with administering a new program can count on increased budgets, higher prestige, and more influence in the power struggles of official Washington. If you support legislation that would establish such a program, you can generally count on the administrating agency's support. Conversely, if your legislation would transfer or even abolish existing programs, you're likely to meet with fervent opposition from the agency currently charged with its administration.

Washington is so complex and the bureaucracy so huge, however, that one agency's discomfiture almost automatically causes elation in another part of the executive branch. If a program currently administered by the Department of Agriculture is killed, bureaucrats at such disparate agencies as the Department of Housing and Urban Development, the Department of Health and Human Services, and even the State Department sometimes secretly rejoice. Just because your objective might be to repeal existing legislation, do not despair of finding allies within the government agencies.

Although several attempts have been made to prohibit government agencies from actively lobbying for or against specific legislation, such laws are a chimera. Most government agencies maintain a staff of "congressional liaison officers"—which are but other words for "lobbyist" in bureaucratese. These officers perform services virtually identical to those of independent lobbyists, but they have vast resources at their disposal, including platoons of researchers who can churn out position papers at the drop of a hat. These people are familiar with all issues related to their agency and often have years of practical experience on the Hill. If you can harness these energies for your purposes, you will have gained thousands of dollars' worth of lobbying at the taxpayers' expense.

Your research should have uncovered the agencies most likely to come to your aid, but you should approach the target agencies gingerly. Most bureaucrats are intensely suspicious of outsiders, and whether they admit it or not, they secretly believe that no one but themselves should really have the right to recommend changes in their agency's operations. This initial suspicion can be dispelled if you emphasize that your interest relates only to final objectives and not necessarily to the manner in which the agency administers the law. Bureaucrats are a much-maligned breed and are as susceptible to criticism (and praise) as anyone else. It is almost always profitable to tell them that you sympathize with their position. One tack is to suggest that they don't currently have the authority to accomplish their mission and your legislation would give them that authority.

Before you approach an executive agency, you should be thoroughly familiar with its organizational structure. Each agency maintains a schematic diagram of its internal chain of command. They are available from the public affairs office or Web site of the agency in question. You should get a copy of this chart for each agency you intend to approach.

Your target should not ordinarily be the congressional liaison office of the agency in question, which rarely has the authority to make policy decisions. Instead, focus on the subdivision of the agency that is currently charged or would be charged with administering the program dealt with in your legislation. If you succeed in securing the subdivision's endorsement, marching orders will pass through an elaborate chain of command to the congressional liaison office. Once that happens, you should work closely with the liaison officers.

Going through the appropriate bureaucratic channels has other benefits as well. The Congress seldom considers legislation without requesting a formal position from the agencies on which it would have a direct effect. You can be instrumental in influencing the statements made by a supportive agency. In a similar vein, the administration as a whole is often asked its position on pending legislation, and the decision as to whether the executive branch will support or oppose a particular bill is often the subject of interagency review. Even if "your" agency is not able to prevail in this review process, its support can at least delay an administration edict, encourage watered-down opposition, or promote neutrality.

In any event, having one or more government departments on your side of a lobbying effort can improve your chances of success. Given the small cost of approaching them, the minimal risk involved if you have done your homework, and the enormous resources they can bring to bear on your side of an issue, a partnership with a federal agency is almost always to be recommended.

A note of caution: because of their highly formalized structure, decision-making within government agencies is ponderous and usually frustrating. Do not expect any agency you approach to provide an affirmative decision overnight. Even when a decision apparently has been made, its implementation may be delayed; the orders may not go out to the congressional liaison officers for days or even weeks after a position has been taken by the policy makers. If you recognize these factors in advance, you are less likely to be disappointed when the agency does not act as expeditiously as you would like.

If you are opposing the position of an agency, the very ponderousness of their decision-making can work to your advantage. You can line up your allies before your "establishment" opposition can even get its troops ready to march.

Other Interest Groups

If you have done your homework, you should also have identified a number of potential allies outside of the government. You should have reviewed all groups with any interest in your ultimate objectives, whether or not they have traditionally opposed your positions. When approaching them, you should have stressed objectives rather than the philosophical motivations of your potential allies.

If you succeed in gaining the support of another group, you should very carefully establish the ground rules. They should be specified in a "memorandum of understanding" that incorporates at least the following factors:

+a clear description of the ultimate objective (e.g., passage or defeat of a particular piece of legislation)

- a list of individuals from each group who will be participating in the lobbying campaign
- a statement identifying which group or individual member thereof (the more specific, the better) will be responsible for preparation of position papers, resource books, and all other written material to be used in the campaign
- procedures by which contacts, error correction, etc. will be implemented
- a provision that establishes a review committee for editing any materials to be used in the campaign so that all interested parties will feel that their position is taken into consideration

You will avoid all sorts of confrontations and misunderstandings if your relationship with your allies is spelled out in detail before you undertake substantive work together. The goals and procedures worked out early in your relationship should be reviewed on a regular basis.

Confrontation often arises when allies think up different ways to accomplish the same objective. The group you're working with can probably draw upon different strengths than those available to your group. You should not insist they merely adopt your methods; rather, give them the freedom to take advantage of their own strengths. Although you may be somewhat uncomfortable with some of their arguments, as long as they cannot be challenged on the basis of accuracy, you should bite your tongue and let it go. The only danger here is *inconsistent* arguments, but they can usually be worked out when you prepare the memorandum of understanding.

Many groups may want to join you, particularly if it appears *you* are going to be successful in your lobbying efforts, but you should be sure that all parties shoulder their share of the burden. It is one thing to work with allies, quite another to carry them.

Members of Congress

The body that you are lobbying—the Congress—can be your greatest source of support. Not only can members vote on your side of the issue, but they also can be instrumental in convincing others to do so. Congressional offices have myriad lobbying devices, many of which are unavailable to outside lobbyists. Among them are

"Dear Colleague" Letters

A letter from one or more members of Congress to their congressional colleagues is a traditional vehicle for expressing views on Capitol Hill. Often, you will have an opportunity to either advise or actually prepare these "dear colleague" letters. Although rather common, they still carry a great deal of weight, particularly if you can get respected members to sign them or if you can attract congressmen and senators of disparate views. Sometimes, several "dear colleague" letters—each emphasizing a different aspect of your issue—are preferable to a single note signed by scores of lawmakers.

Committees and Party Organizations

Members of Congress have direct access to various restricted forums. They can make their views known in groups to which you would ordinarily be denied access. If a member is committed to your cause, you can suggest that he or she use all such privileges to promote your position.

Other Interest Groups

It is rare that another lobbyist would flatly refuse a request from a congressman or senator. After all, the lobbyist has a lot of favors to ask the member in return. If you need a particular ally in the private sector, one of the best ways to approach that person is to have a friendly congressman or senator make the initial contact.

Log Rolling

Whatever the didactic skills of friendly members of Congress, their ability to convince colleagues of the objective merits of your issue may be somewhat less impressive than their political power. If members feel strongly about your issue, they can use all manner of resources to convince their brethren to go along with them. Their methods range from straight vote trading to using their influence as chairman of a committee or subcommittee, caucus, state delegation, party post, etc. Although trading votes may seem somewhat sordid, it is a tradition in American politics and is just as much a part of lobbying as a letter-writing campaign.

　　If you secure a member of Congress as your lobbying ally, you should be prepared to help that member in any way he or she requires—for example, by preparing position papers or research. Keep in mind that you will not be able to control what a member of Congress says or does nearly as well as you would your own people. This can be embarrassing, but the risk is worth it. A friendly member can do much more good than harm to your cause.

Endorsements

Some lobbying campaigns spend a great deal of time and effort attempting to get as many groups as possible to endorse their positions. Although endorsements are worthwhile, they are often overrated. A long list of organizations supporting your position can be impressive and lends a certain amount of credibility to your cause, particularly in areas in which you are not especially strong, but unless the groups endorsing you are also willing to do active lobbying, you cannot expect their names to carry the day. It is better to have three groups that will give you time, effort, money, and manpower than thirty that will merely lend you the use of their name. Given limited resources, you should spend much more time attempting to convince people to work with you than trying to get them to merely approve of what you are saying.

In seeking endorsements, you should make it very clear to the groups you contact that you want to use their names publicly. It can be devastating if a group that you claim has endorsed your position subsequently repudiates the endorsement. You should keep the group's leaders updated on the manner in which you use the group's name; send them copies of all documents in which the name appears. If they have declined to do more than merely sanction the use of their organization's title, it is not generally necessary for you to clear the text of every single document with them. You should, however, be very careful not to misrepresent their endorsement. In particular, make sure their name is used only in connection with the areas that were discussed in your original conversations. For example, it is not unusual for a labor union to endorse corporate management's position on such issues as tariff protection, but it would be inaccurate to imply that the labor union agrees with management on *other* issues as a result. One particularly effective way of coordinating other groups' endorsements is to arrange for them to post a supporting position on their Web site and cross-linking that statement with your own site.

On the other hand, your group should never endorse a lobbying campaign sponsored by another organization unless you plan to take an active part in the promotion of that group's cause. From your perspective, endorsements gain you no followers, and the political points you may earn with other groups are ephemeral at best. Finally, your future credibility should never be entrusted to another organization unless you have the ability to control the statements made in your name.

13
MONEY

Get thee glass eyes;
And, like a scurvy politician, seem
To see the things thou dost not. . . .

—William Shakespeare, *King Lear*

Money is the mother's milk of politics. To succeed, you must be able to effectively raise funds for your cause and utilize those funds wisely. How to do so is the most controversial issue you'll face as a lobbyist.

The Law

Before you embark on a lobbying campaign, you should familiarize yourself with the laws that regulate how money may be raised and spent to influence political causes. The federal government has always attempted to steer a narrow path between turning a blind eye to corruption and infringing upon First Amendment rights. While (almost) everyone is opposed to graft, most would also agree that an outright ban on using money to express a political opinion would be unconstitutional. For example, zoning laws aside, few would challenge a citizen's right to put a sign in his or her yard advocating the election (or defeat) of a particular candidate. The Congress has wrestled many times with this conundrum, vacillating between mere "transparency laws," which require divulging the source of funds and their expenditure, to outright bans on certain types of spending.

The most pertinent laws for the lobbyist are the Lobbying Disclosure Act of 1995 (which repealed the Federal Regulation of Lobbying Act, passed in 1946) and the Federal Election Campaign Act, passed in 1971. The Lobbying Disclosure Act has remained unamended since its passage, whereas the Federal Election Campaign Act has been amended periodically, most recently with the

Bipartisan Campaign Reform Act of 2002 (also called the McCain-Feingold Act). In addition, both the Senate and the House have a Code of Official Conduct, which has a direct bearing on how money may be used or accepted, and the Legislative Transparency and Accountability Act is likely to become law in some form in the immediate future.

The Lobbying Disclosure Act

Section 4 of the Lobbying Disclosure Act states: "No later than 45 days after a lobbyist first makes a lobbying contact or is employed or retained to make a lobbying contact, whichever is earlier, such lobbyist . . . shall register with the Secretary of the Senate and the Clerk of the House of Representatives."

In passing the LDA, the Congress recognized the inadequacies of previous lobbying legislation (such as the Federal Regulation of Lobbying Act) and provided clearer guidelines as to who is required to register and what they are required to disclose. In essence, a person must register as a lobbyist if he or she is retained by a client to interact with certain members of the executive and/or legislative branch with regard to the formulation, modification, or adoption of federal legislation, rules, regulations, executive orders, or positions. This interaction is defined as a "lobbying contact." Section 3(8)(B) carves out numerous exceptions to this definition, so it would be wise to carefully read that section.

A person needs to register as a lobbyist only if he or she makes more than one lobbying contact, devotes more than 20 percent of the time spent working for a client on lobbying activities, and receives more than five thousand dollars from the client in a six-month period. Organizations (including nonprofits) must register if they spend more than twenty thousand dollars on lobbying activities and employ at least one person who makes more than one lobbying contact and devotes more than 20 percent of the time spent working for a client on lobbying activities. The same rules apply if the lobbyist's "client" is his or her own organization. If the lobbyist or organization has more than one client, separate registration needs to be filled out for each client. If the lobbyist or organization makes multiple lobbying contacts for one client, one registration encompassing all the contacts will suffice.

The act specifies two major responsibilities for the lobbyist. The first is to keep a detailed and exact account of

(1) the name, address, business telephone number, and principal place of business of the registrant, and a general description of its business or activities;

(2) the name, address, and principal place of business of the registrant's client, and a general description of its business or activities (if different from paragraph (1));

(3) the name, address, and principal place of business of any organization, other than the client, that—
  (A) contributes more than $10,000 toward the lobbying activities of the registrant in a semiannual period . . . ; and
  (B) in whole or in major part plans, supervises, or controls such lobbying activities.

(4) the name, address, principal place of business, amount of any contribution of more than $10,000 to the lobbying activities of the registrant, and approximate percentage of equitable ownership in the client (if any) of any foreign entity that—
  (A) holds at least 20 percent equitable ownership in the client or any organization identified under paragraph (3);
  (B) directly or indirectly, in whole or in major part, plans, supervises, controls, directs, finances, or subsidizes the activities of the client or any organization identified under paragraph (3); or
  (C) is an affiliate of the client or any organization identified under paragraph (3) and has a direct interest in the outcome of the lobbying activity;

(5) a statement of—
  (A) the general issue areas in which the registrant expects to engage in lobbying activities on behalf of the client; and
  (B) to the extent practicable, specific issues that have (as of the date of the registration) already been addressed or are likely to be addressed in lobbying activities; and

(6) the name of each employee of the registrant who has acted or whom the registrant expects to act as a lobbyist on behalf of the client and, if any such employee has served as a covered executive branch official or a covered legislative branch official in the 2 years before the date on which such employee first acted (after the date of enactment of this Act) as a lobbyist on behalf of the client, the position in which such employee served.

The second major requirement for the lobbyist is to file the following information with the secretary of the Senate and the clerk of the House of Representatives "no later than 45 days after the end of the semiannual period beginning on the first day of each January and the first day of July":

(1) the name of the registrant, the name of the client, and any changes or updates to the information provided in the initial registration;
(2) for each general issue area in which the registrant engaged in lobbying activities on behalf of the client during the semiannual filing period—

(A) a list of the specific issues upon which a lobbyist employed by the registrant engaged in lobbying activities, including, to the maximum extent practicable, a list of bill numbers and references to specific executive branch actions;

(B) a statement of the Houses of Congress and the Federal agencies contacted by lobbyists employed by the registrant on behalf of the client;

(C) a list of the employees of the registrant who acted as lobbyists on behalf of the client; and

(D) a description of the interest, if any, of any foreign entity identified under section 4(b)(4) in the specific issues listed under subparagraph (A);

(3) in the case of a lobbying firm, a good faith estimate of the total amount of all income from the client (including any payments to the registrant by any other person for lobbying activities on behalf of the client) during the semiannual period, other than income for matters that are unrelated to lobbying activities; and

(4) in the case of a registrant engaged in lobbying activities on its own behalf, a good faith estimate of the total expenses that the registrant and its employees incurred in connection with lobbying activities during the semiannual filing period.

The above requirements are the most important strictures of the Lobbying Disclosure Act, but it cannot be stressed enough that you should become completely familiar with the provisions of this act. Noncompliance is a misdemeanor that could result in a fine of up to fifty thousand dollars.

The Federal Election Campaign Act

The Federal Election Campaign Act contains provisions regarding contributions made to influence the results of an election. The type of contribution that is most pertinent to lobbyists is the "independent expenditure." The Bipartisan Campaign Reform Act amends the act's definition of an "independent expenditure" to

an expenditure by a person expressly advocating the election or defeat of a clearly identified candidate . . . that is not made in concert or cooperation with or at the request or suggestion of such candidate, the candidate's authorized political committee, or their agents, or a political party committee or its agents.

Other provisions of the act limit the amount of money that can be donated to a particular candidate or political committee. Individuals may contribute according to the guidelines set out below; however, except in very specific situations, the Campaign Act prohibits a corporation from making a contribution or expenditure in connection with any election to any political office. An organization that wishes to contribute to political campaigns must either encourage its members to contribute individually to particular candidates, or form a political action committee (PAC) to collect and distribute its members' donations. There are currently hundreds of PACs, representing everything from major corporations to special interest groups.

Establishing a political action committee of your own can give you much better control of where your group's contributions are going and concentrate your political influence. The rules for creating and operating a PAC are explicitly delineated in the Federal Election Campaign Act and Bipartisan Campaign Reform Act. PACs are easy and inexpensive to set up—they usually cost from three to five hundred dollars—but you should have an attorney assist you with their establishment. The Federal Election Commission also provides free information on the establishment and operation of PACs on its Web site, www.fec.gov.

The chart on the following page illustrates the contribution limits for PACs, individuals, and others as of this writing. These limits will change over time, so be sure to check with the FEC before writing any checks.

Gifts to Congressmen, Senators, and Staffs

Disregard what you may have heard about members of Congress on the take. With the exception of contributions to congressional campaigns, which we will discuss in the next section, you should be very reticent in giving either gifts or money to members of Congress and their staffs. Many offices will simply not accept gifts; others will do so only under extremely restricted conditions.

There are, however, several types of gifts that are accepted lobbying tactics. They include

Books

For some reason books are not looked upon as gifts if they relate to your issue and can be regarded as "educational material." For example, a book on wilderness might be gladly accepted by a congressman or senator who has assisted you in a land-use matter. Even expensive coffee-table books are routinely accepted by some of the most fastidious people on the Hill.

Contribution Limits 2007–2008

	To each candidate or candidate committee per election	To national party committee per calendar year	To state, district & local party committee per calendar year	To any other political committee per calendar year[1]	Special Limits
Individual may give	$2,300*	$28,500*	$10,000 (combined limit)	$5,000	$108,200* overall biennial limit: •$42,700* to all candidates •$65,500* to all PACs and parties[2]
National Party Committee may give	$5,000	No limit	No limit	$5,000	$39,900* to Senate candidate per campaign[3]
State, District & Local Party Committee may give	$5,000 (combined limit)	No limit	No limit	$5,000 (combined limit)	No limit
PAC (multi-candidate)[4] may give	$5,000	$15,000	$5,000 (combined limit)	$5,000	No limit
PAC (not multi-candidate) may give	$2,300*	$28,500*	$10,000 (combined limit)	$5,000	No limit
Authorized Campaign Committee may give	$2,000[5]	No limit	No limit	$5,000	No limit

Source: Federal Election Commission, *Contributions Brochure*, February 2004 (updated January 2007), www.fec-gov/pages/brochures/contrib.shtml.

---

* These contribution limits are increased for inflation in odd-numbered years.

1. A contribution earmarked for a candidate through a political committee counts against the original contributor's limit for that candidate. In certain circumstances, the contribution may also count against the contributor's limit to the PAC. . . .

2. No more than $42,700 of this amount may be contributed to state and local party committees and PACs.

3. This limit is shared by the national committee and the Senate campaign committee.

4. A multicandidate committee is a political committee with more than 50 contributors which has been registered for at least 6 months and, with the exception of state party committees, has made contributions to 5 or more candidates for federal office. . . .

5. A federal candidate's authorized committee(s) may contribute no more than $2,000 per election to another federal candidate's authorized committee(s). . . .

Ethics rules require a small precaution, however. Before giving a relevant book to a member of Congress, you must inscribe it with the member's name and the name of your organization. For example:

> To the Hon. Libby Lovetree:
>
> The American people appreciate your efforts to preserve liberty. We are sure a champion of this cause such as you could have written it herself, but we hope that you can use it to educate other members of Congress.
>
> Flat Earth Society
> November 2007

Gifts Under Five Dollars

The cutoff point between a gift and a bribe is five dollars—you can never be accused of bribing a member of Congress for what amounts to Metro fare. You will have little occasion to actually give members or their staffers cash, but gifts of pens, pencils, and paperweights with a value of five dollars or so is routine in Washington. Even if the value is slightly over five dollars, you should not have a problem. Beware, however, of giving away radios, television sets, or the like; that is the fastest way of making it into the scandal sheets or bloggers' screeds, and that you don't need.

Awards

Members of Congress love to receive awards with which to adorn their offices. Dozens of groups routinely bestow awards upon congressmen and senators who have supported their views. Sometimes, these awards are elaborate (and expensive) plaques extolling the virtues of the member. It is essential, however, that the award be inscribed with the member's name, to conform to ethics guidelines.

As long as the award is not cash or a useful consumer item, don't worry too much about cost—within the bounds of good taste. Obviously, for example, a solid-gold loving cup worth fifteen thousand dollars would not be appropriate.

Liquor

At Christmastime, congressional offices seem to appreciate the holiday spirit. Liquor has sometimes been considered an acceptable gift at that time of year. Usually, it is used for office parties, the cost of which would otherwise come out of the member's budget. However, given recent changes to the ethics rules, most congressional offices now have strict policies against accepting these kinds of offerings. It is always safer to assume that gifts of liquor are prohibited unless you have discreetly checked with the member's personal secretary or AA in advance and received specific and unequivocal approval.

Even if you receive the go-ahead, don't overdo it. Although some lobbyists give away entire cases to senators and congressmen, you should limit yourself to two or three bottles. There is much less chance of criticism about a bottle of scotch than a whole case of Jack Daniel's.

In some cases, a congressional office may have policies against taking liquor but the member's campaign committee will gladly accept it. In this circumstance, merely drop off your gift at the member's office and request that it be delivered to the committee. (Be sure to leave your business card—it's good politics, and they can get the information they need to report to the FEC from the card.)

Models, Samples, Etc.

Many industrial trade associations routinely distribute models or samples of their products to member of Congress of whom they are constituents. Although these models and samples are sometimes worth hundreds of dollars, they are rarely functional. When you get to the Hill you will see such objects displayed in congressional offices, so there obviously is not much resistance to them. Again, however, these gifts must be inscribed with the member's name. They should also be approved in advance by the member's AA, and one of the member's staffers should check with the Senate or House Ethics Committee to verify their appropriateness. The staffer should ask the committee how the member could accept your proffered gifts within the law and request a letter stating the committee's opinion. If the committee indicates that the gifts are acceptable, be sure to get a copy of its letter for your files.

The Ethics Committees in both the Senate and the House are set up to protect members from unethical conduct, as well as to discipline members who violate the rules. In many cases, committee counsel can provide the member and you with proper clearance, but it is important you receive it in writing before you make what could be an embarrassing mistake. The recent changes to the ethics rules of the House and Senate are not only tricky but also do not address all the possibilities for the "appearance of impropriety." Since the revised rules were written, they have been reinterpreted almost monthly; the clear language of the rules is not a good guide to what is acceptable. *Do not guess.* Ask the member's staff to request an opinion before proceeding.

You should exercise even greater care if you would like to give a member a more suspicious gift, such as free travel, hunting or golfing trips, theater tickets, or stock.

Charity Events

Some organizations arrange for congressional appearances at what are ostensibly "charity events." This practice often involves bringing a member (and sometimes his or her spouse) to a resort location in the member's state or district where the member gives a brief speech and a donation is made to a local charity in his or her name. Many members love these events. Not only do they get to meet some high rollers (and potential contributors), but they also get credit among their own constituents for delivering the bacon to a worthy cause. Since neither they nor their campaign committees have received a dime in cash or in-kind contributions, these events can generally pass ethical muster. However, given the Hill's sensitivity regarding ethical standards these days, it is not only prudent but downright essential that the specific arrangements for such charity events be cleared by the appropriate Ethics Committee before they are implemented.

Campaign Contributions

Contributions to congressional campaigns are regulated by a plethora of federal laws that are complex and constantly changing, and it is beyond the scope of this book to consider all the technicalities. The general rules outlined below are merely practical guidelines—not legal advice. For the latest on campaign finance law, you should visit the Federal Election Commission Web site (www.fec.gov).

Laws governing campaign contributions are almost as complex as the tax statutes and are a minefield for the unwary. Even with donations other than the traditional cash contribution, the rules can be confusing. If, for example, an individual's regular employer gives him or her a leave of absence (beyond the regular vacation or leave period) to work in a congressional campaign, this can be construed as a "contribution in kind" to the candidate from the employer (and in some circumstances, from the employee as well) and must be declared in the candidate's report to the Federal Election Commission. Similarly, if the owner of a meeting hall generally charges a fee for the rental of the facility but allows a candidate to hold a political rally there for free, that gesture may be regarded as a contribution in kind. If a car rental firm gives a member of Congress free use of one of its vehicles during a campaign, this act might not only be regarded as a contribution in kind, but also declared an illegal violation of corporate contribution statutes. (On the other hand, if a volunteer campaign worker uses his or her own car to transport other volunteers to and from campaign headquarters or to political rallies, it would not ordinarily be regarded as a contribution in kind.) In certain circumstances, the use of your organization's own office can be regarded as a contribution in kind.

When it comes to the laws concerning campaign contributions, you should not merely trust your good judgment; the law, as almost everyone knows, is not always logical. And even if your contribution is within the law, many congressional offices have their own restrictions. For example, a few refuse to accept funds from political action committees, and some restrict all contributions over a specified amount. The rules can be frustrating, but you can avoid most of the pitfalls if you adopt the following procedures:

Consult with the Campaign Treasurer

If your group decides to make donations to a campaign, particularly if it involves anything other than a straight cash contribution, you should first check with the candidate's campaign treasurer to determine the legality and appropriateness of the gift. You should also insist upon a letter from the campaign treasurer that specifies the nature of the gift, confirms that the treasurer has made a determination such gift is legal, and promises that it will be appropriately reported.

Make Donations Directly to the Campaign Committee

Payments to a candidate of cash or other things of value are almost always illegal unless they are directly related to campaign financing. Although there are a number of exceptions to this rule, you should try to avoid them; you cannot afford to risk ruining the reputation of your organization or your issue by taking unnecessary chances. Your immutable rule should be that cash gifts over five dollars can be made only to campaign committees, never to a candidate personally or to his or her staff.

As for non-cash contributions, there are a number of technical loopholes in the Federal Election Campaign Act and in the ethics rules of both the House and Senate, but these exceptions are so narrow that you should not attempt to use them unless specifically requested to do so by a member of Congress and unless you have a firm written legal opinion from an attorney that such exceptions are appropriate.

Never Give Actual Cash

It may be legal to provide a donation in the form of bank notes, coins, stock, or other apparently untraceable monetary instruments, but such contributions make record-keeping difficult and are inherently suspicious. All contributions to a political campaign should be by personal check or a check from a PAC or its equivalent. Corporate checks, partnership checks, labor union checks, etc., should never be used, even though they may be technically legal under certain very restricted circumstances.

There are some circumstances, however, in which you or your organization may have "real" money that you wish to contribute—for instance, if you have a fundraiser (for example, a picnic) and someone passes the hat for a candidate's campaign. At the end of the day you may wind up with two or three hundred used dollar bills with no indication where they came from. In this situation, do not merely ship off the loot to the candidate's campaign committee. If you've established a political action committee, you can deposit the money to your PAC and send an official check to the campaign for the collected amount, but if you don't have a PAC, the situation becomes more complicated. A responsible individual should count the money, deposit it in his or her own checking account, and write a check to the campaign committee for that amount. The personal check should be sent to the campaign committee with a letter of explanation, which might run as follows:

Congressman Lloyd Kreeger
Kreeger for Congress Committee
1416 Pearl Street
Boulder, Colorado 80302

Dear Congressman Kreeger:

Attached is my personal check for $246.00 for your reelection campaign. This sum represents the amount collected at the Flat Earth Society Annual Picnic last week. Jim Barstow passed the hat for you and almost everyone there chipped in a dollar or two. Everyone in the Boulder County chapter was invited, and I attach a membership list for your files. I deposited the money in my account and the attached check represents the total of all the cash contributions. I hope this procedure is acceptable to your campaign committee. If your campaign treasurer has any questions, please have him contact me directly.

As you know, all of us in the Boulder County Flat Earth Society strongly support you.

Sincerely,
Alice Goosebumple
Secretary/Treasurer

Some campaign treasurers are leery of accepting cash even through this indirect method, but at least they have your letter of explanation to clarify their records.

Although this method will work in a pinch, it is almost always better to give a campaign committee fifty $5 checks from individual members than a consolidated check for $250, for several reasons. Campaigns like to tout that they are supported by "the little guy," which they demonstrate by publicizing how many small gifts they receive. Personal checks also identify supporters, whose names are extremely valuable to any campaign. Finally, there is a political axiom that people who have given money—even $5—have a stake in the outcome of the election and rarely go over to the other side.

Report and Document Contributions Accurately

The major trap into which many groups fall is not that they make illegal contributions per se, but that they fail to adequately report what are otherwise permissible gifts. In most cases, contributions to campaign committees must be reported by the committees themselves; you need do nothing more than tell the campaign committee the name, address, telephone number, occupation, employer, contribution amount, and contribution date for each donor. Most congressional campaign committees can provide preprinted contribution cards for this purpose, but if you do not have access to them, you should be sure to advise all your members to include this information on a separate piece of paper when they send in their contributions. This saves the campaign committee the time and expense of having to request it later.

If you or any member of your group intends to give more than a few hundred dollars to a particular candidate, however, certain additional reporting steps may be required. Timeliness is very important; reports are required no later than 24 hours after the contribution is received. Do not merely read the Federal Election Campaign Act and decide on your own if a contribution needs to be reported; that law is reinterpreted so often that you must rely on legal counsel for the most up-to-date regulatory status—particularly when dealing with non-cash contributions. As noted previously, all sorts of donations to a campaign may be regarded as contributions in kind, and they may need be reported.

Don't take chances. Both you and the candidate could be embarrassed by unreported or insufficiently documented contributions. If you have any doubt about whether a donation must be reported or how it should be reported, contact the treasurer of the applicable campaign committee for a legal opinion concerning appropriate reporting procedures.

The more thoroughly you are able to document your expenditures, the less concern you need have about compliance with the Federal Election Campaign Act and other applicable statutes. Set up books according to accepted accounting principles. Not only is this a good business practice, but it will enable you to comply with future reporting rules that have not yet been devised.

You should also be diligent about keeping records of the contributions made by members of your group. This information has great political value that can be used later. Tell your members, either in one of your regular newsletters or in a special letter or e-mail, that each time they make a contribution they should let you know the name of the recipient and the amount donated so that you can keep a tally sheet. This is particularly important if your organization has decided to endorse particular candidates for public office. You need to know how effective your fundraising efforts have been so you can claim appropriate credit from the congressman or senator.

Dealing with money is one of the most complex areas of lobbying. Even if you don't like lawyers, you should talk to them early in your efforts. It is cheaper to talk to your lawyer now than their lawyer later.

Nonpolitical Contributions

Because election and ethics laws are so stringent, many lobbying groups focus instead on *nonpolitical* expenditures that are not affected by either the Federal Election Campaign Act or any of the ethics rules. Such expenditures can include paying to advertise your issue (as opposed to endorsing particular candidates) in the media, contributing to nonpolitical organizations that share your views, and sponsoring public interest activities such as "get out the vote" campaigns (as long as you are not acting on behalf of a particular candidate).

Sometimes the difference between political and nonpolitical expenditures is a subtle one. For example, if a group ranks members of Congress according to their voting records on issues relevant to its cause, this act is generally regarded as nonpolitical, even if the ranking is published at the group's expense in major newspapers. This type of thing must be done very carefully, however, or it can get you into trouble. Get a legal opinion letter from an attorney before you publish your rankings.

Nonpolitical contributions are so prevalent that some public interest groups have denounced them as de facto loopholes in the campaign laws. These groups argue that the distinction between political and nonpolitical is so vague that ethics and election laws should be expanded to cover so-called nonpolitical contributions. The danger in enacting a truly comprehensive statute to prohibit or regulate such expenditures is obvious—the Constitution guarantees citizens the right to petition the government. A comprehensive statute would have to regulate even individuals writing to congressmen on their own behalf or flying to Washington to see their senators. An individual taxpayer might be prohibited from taking out an ad in the local newspaper denouncing a property tax increase, or a group might be barred from publicly displaying its views on a billboard. Such restrictions would fly in the face of First Amendment guarantees of freedom of expression and would almost surely be struck down by the courts.

The general rule to follow with regard to nonpolitical contributions is that the expenditure of money on promotion of an issue rather than a candidate for public office is a right almost universally guaranteed by the Constitution.

When, How, and How Much to Give to Whom

One factor that discourages many groups from making political contributions is the inordinately high cost of campaigns. Today, even minor congressional campaigns cost upward of six hundred thousand dollars. Faced with those kinds of expenditures, many groups wonder whether it is worth contributing at all, given their limited resources. The obvious answer is yes. The question is really to whom.

A group is usually better advised to make twelve one-hundred-dollar contributions than one twelve-hundred-dollar contribution; it is not necessary for you or your group to give thousands of dollars to a single candidate in order to be noticed. On the other hand, an organization might be regarded as downright miserly if it provided only five dollars to a particular candidate's reelection campaign. (This rule does not apply to individuals, whose five-dollar contributions are welcomed by most campaigns as a sign of solid grassroots support.) In general, it is most appropriate for an organization to contribute one hundred to five hundred dollars to a single campaign.

Your first step in determining whom your group will support is to analyze the state of your finances. If you have only two hundred dollars, you should concentrate on two or, at most, three candidates. As your finances improve, you gain more flexibility in the number of people you can support.

After you have determined the number of campaign contributions your group can make, your next priority should be to decide who the recipients will be. In general, it is a good rule to stand by your friends. Thus, you should give the highest priority to members of Congress who have not only voted on your side of your issue, but also actively assisted in promoting your cause. If there are a number of equally deserving candidates, you should give to the ones with whom you have the strongest constituent ties. If you have any money left after making these contributions, give to incumbent members of Congress who have supported your position. Finally, if you still have some money to spare, consider gifts to challengers of your strongest opponents. It is extremely unwise, however, to merely attempt to defeat your opponents without first determining what position their replacements would take on your issue. Before you make a contribution to a challenger, be sure you have his or her support. It is also much more important to retain your friends than to attempt to defeat enemies, particularly given the limited resources of most grassroots lobbying campaigns.

You should never contribute to both candidates in a campaign in the hope of currying favor with whoever wins. Since campaign contributions are a matter of public record, most candidates will check their opponent's contributors. You will not fool anybody if you try to play both sides of the street; you will merely squander your resources.

However limited your contribution funds, you can maximize the effectiveness of your contributions through proper timing. Most contributors wait until the polls show a clear leader in an election before they spend their money. Members of Congress know this, and although even late dollars are appreciated, early money is the most desirable. Since so few people contribute early, congressmen and senators who read the lists are likely to remember those who do. You are almost always better off making your decision early in an election year and contributing at least half your total gifts before the primary elections. You will make more of an impression that way.

Raising Money

Fundraising is one of the most complex aspects of politics from both a legal and a practical point of view. Most campaign committees prefer that you establish a PAC and then donate the money to them rather than act as a third-party fundraiser for the committee itself, but both options are discussed below.

PAC Fundraising

If you take the safer and more effective approach of forming a political action committee, you can ask your members to contribute not to candidates, but to the PAC itself. A sample fundraising letter might read as follows:

Dear Fellow Flat Earth Believer:

Did you know that legislation that would virtually abolish Flat Earthism as a matter of federal law is currently pending in the Congress? Did you know that this legislation already has fifty cosponsors? Did you know that your tax dollars will be used to attack your beliefs?

Most of you are aware of these facts, but don't know what to do about it. The best way to stop spending your tax dollars to kill your own beliefs is to invest in lawmakers who truly represent your feelings. Today, dozens of Flat Earth congressmen and senators have been targeted by Round Earthers who want to abolish Flat Earthism with your own money. We simply must stop them.

The Round Earthers are putting together "war chests" totaling hundreds of thousands of dollars to deny you representation in the Congress. You could, of course, contribute to one or two congressmen or senators who share your views, but if you are like most of us, you don't have the means to match the big money of Round Earthers. There is one alternative: by combining hundreds of small $5 and $10 contributions, the Flat Earth Political Action Committee (FLATPAC) can concentrate its resources on the key campaigns to save our friends on Capitol Hill from the Round Earth attack. Together, we can concentrate our resources on the really critical races to make sure our voice is heard.

FLATPAC is composed of people just like you and me who are concerned about the direction our country is taking and want to preserve Flat Earthism as a fundamental right of belief.

Won't you please help us today by enclosing your $5, $10, $25, or $50 contribution? The future of Flat Earthism depends on you.

Sincerely,
Bret Collins, Chairman
FLATPAC

Be sure to include a reporting sheet with this solicitation that donors will complete when sending their contribution. As mentioned above, the reporting sheet should include at least the following:

Name_____
Address_____
Telephone_____
Employer_____
Amount of Contribution_____
Date_____

Of course, you can request additional information for your own purposes, but the above data is what must be reported to the FEC.

Third-Party Fundraising

Some lobbying groups avoid legal questions entirely by merely acting as a surrogate for campaigns they recommend. This method is used particularly by "527" organizations. These 527 groups, named after Section 527 of the IRS Tax Code, technically do not spend their own money to directly advocate the election or defeat of any candidate for federal elective office, so they avoid regulation by the Federal Elections Commission. This is one of the clever methods used to avoid the technical proscriptions of campaign finance laws.

The third-party fundraiser sends a letter similar to the one above. Rather than soliciting contributions to a PAC, however, the letter requests that the reader contribute directly to a candidate's campaign committee. It specifies the committee to which checks should be made out, but the group takes care of the logistics in actually delivering the checks. The FEC form (above) is still required.

Before you raise money for any particular candidate in this way, you should seek explicit written advice from the treasurer of the candidate's campaign. Be familiar with all legal requirements.

Outside Consultants

In addition to sending fundraising letters, your PAC or third-party fundraising group should use every other means of reaching potential contributors. Some groups retain outside consultants to assist them in mass-mailing efforts. If you decide to do this, you should get a very good idea of cost before signing a contract. In addition to the consultant's fee, administrative and mailing costs often amount to phenomenal sums of money and return only a few cents on every dollar collected in contributions, unless you maintain very tight control. Be particularly leery of promoters who promise to raise millions of dollars. The question is not how much they raise, but how much they keep. After expenses, a well-managed campaign that raises $100,000 may keep $80,000. Another campaign may raise $250,000 but net only $40,000.

This is not to suggest that mass-mailing campaigns are not useful, if only to put your name in front of the public, but they are not a panacea for empty coffers.

The Fundraiser

When you decide to contribute to a particular member or challenger, you should attempt to get the most for your dollar—including an invitation to a congressional fundraiser. These fundraisers, usually held in Washington or the home state or district, are where most congressional campaigns raise the bulk of their money. Lobbyists are generally given one free ticket for each contribution (often in the one-to-two-hundred-dollar range). For that kind of money, you might expect at least some pretty good food; don't bet on it. The purpose of the fundraiser is just that. Every cent spent on cold shrimp comes right out of the campaign.

How to Be Invited

If you have one hundred dollars to spend, it is easy to be invited to a fundraiser. Merely call the candidate's congressional office (for an incumbent) or the party headquarters in the candidate's state (for a challenger) and ask to be added to the "contribution list." You will certainly be invited to the next reception. When the invitation arrives, it is invariably impressive. Usually it will appear to be a request from other members of Congress (generally ranking members of the candidate's party) that you attend a reception in the candidate's honor. Don't believe it. The reception is being held by the candidate's campaign committee. The "hosts" will make a token appearance and leave after about five minutes.

How to Accept an Invitation

The invitation will include an RSVP card and a return envelope. The RSVP card is not merely a courtesy. It is with this card that you will submit your contribution check; the card itself will request the reporting information for the FEC. Fill it out—but if the candidate is an incumbent, do not return it in the envelope provided. That envelope will be addressed to the candidate's campaign headquarters, where it may never be seen by the candidate or his or her regular staff; send it instead to the candidate's congressional office. If your candidate is a challenger, it is OK to send it to the campaign headquarters—although if he or she holds public office elsewhere, you may wish to send it to the appropriate office address. In any case, however, don't just drop it in the mail. Write a letter, attaching the RSVP card and your check, made out to the campaign committee. The letter should be very informal and should not mention issues. Such a letter might be as follows:

> Dear Congresswoman Lumpen:
>
> Enclosed is a small contribution for your campaign. All of us in the Flat Earth Society are pulling for you.
>   I'm looking forward to seeing you on the nineteenth.
>
> Sincerely,
> Bob Bunkhead
> Flat Earth Society of Cleveland

If you send this letter to the candidate's office address, his or her regular staff will forward your RSVP card to the campaign committee (to which the original return envelope was addressed), but since there is money attached, there is a good chance they will read your letter. By following this procedure, you have put your name—and the name of your group—before the people who count. Note that this gambit works only if you have at least two weeks between the time you mail your letter and the reception. Last-minute mailings are doomed to delay, particularly on the Hill, where current security precautions have slowed mail delivery to a crawl.

Arriving at the Fundraiser

Your check is in the mail. You arrive at the reception. The first thing you encounter is a table with staffers behind it. Give them your name; they will check you off the master list of persons from whom they have received contributions. If you have sent your money but your name is not on the list, or if they have no record of having received your contribution, you can save yourself a lot of embarrassment by writing another check on the spot and making a stop payment request on the first check with your bank the next day. Be sure to tell the staffer at the door that is what you intend to do and wait to see that he or she makes a note of it so the office won't be surprised when the first check shows up (and then bounces). Delays in receiving (or recording) your contribution are fairly common, particularly if you send the check to the regular office address as suggested above.

At most receptions, guests will be given name tags. Put yours on your right side (it's easier to read when shaking hands with someone).

There will usually be a reception line with the candidate, his or her spouse, a staffer, and perhaps even one of the hosts. Don't expect Amy Vanderbilt protocol at one of these receptions. This is politics, not a debutante ball. Be brief in the receiving line; remind the candidate and the staffer of your name and organization. You'll get a few minutes to chat with the candidate later in the reception if you're aggressive enough.

Liquor and Food

Head for the food or the bar, according to your own preference. A word about drinking: although the liquor is free at a fundraiser, the serious lobbyist should realize that it is not a social event in the usual sense of the term. It is a business function. You'll be discussing serious issues and that becomes difficult if you've had too much to drink. Your reputation, and that of your issue, may well be judged by your actions, and people aren't inclined to take drunks seriously— have one or, at the most, two small drinks. If you aren't comfortable unless you have something that looks strong in your hand, order a Virgin Mary, a tonic on the rocks, or a lime and Coke. People don't drink milk at fundraisers unless they are trying to impress a congressman from Wisconsin.

Don't expect to satisfy a ravenous hunger at a fundraiser. Usually the fare will consist of canapés and other hors d'oeuvres. Have one or two and reserve a table at a nearby restaurant for later.

Circulating

Most of the other people at the fundraiser will be lobbyists, too. All, or almost all, will be friendly, harassed, tired, and slightly egotistical—but they can be a gold mine of information. They are easy to meet at receptions such as this and, despite some huddles in the corners, they enjoy circulating. Meet as many as possible by asking what problems they are working on. Usually, they'll be more than happy to tell you.

Watch for the breakup of the receiving line; that signals that the candidate is going to circulate. Position yourself in a convenient place, and politely but firmly see to it that you get the candidate's attention.

Always start out by thanking the candidate for inviting you, and remind him or her of your group. Next, say how much you appreciate the candidate's support on your issue (even if he or she has waffled on it from time to time). Finally, tell the candidate that you intend to go back to your group and encourage all of them to support him or her (there are ten thousand ways to do this). Get the above points into your conversation, but don't state them as crassly as noted above.

Be sure to give the candidate one of your business cards (see chapter 11, "What to Say and How to Say It"). Give a card to the accompanying staffer, too. If the staff is at all efficient, the cards will eventually find their way into the candidate's cross-index files.

Don't discuss the detailed points of your issue with the candidate at the fundraiser unless he or she asks you a specific question. Detailed discussions are much more appropriate and more useful during office hours. Before you leave, ask the candidate or the staffer for an appointment, unless you just visited that week. He or she will undoubtedly agree, but will be vague on timing. (This will be the case even if the candidate is a challenger rather than incumbent; in fact, challengers are even more likely to meet with you, since their sole concern is getting elected, while a sitting member still has those pesky constitutional duties to perform.) Tell the candidate you are tentatively free about three days hence, and that you will call his or her secretary to confirm. Be sure the staffer is made aware of this. You will go to the staffer—not the candidate—if the personal secretary is reluctant to arrange the meeting when you call.

Fundraisers are generally held on Tuesday, Wednesday, or Thursday in the late afternoon or early evening. It is considered somewhat bad form to be among the last to leave the party, so you should plan on staying about an hour or so—not until the bar closes.

At these functions, you'll often find other lobbyists or staffers with interests similar to yours. If you feel up to it, invite them for a light dinner. Meeting other lobbyists builds your network of contacts, and in Washington, building your network—both in and out of government—is the most precious currency you can have next to your own credibility. A healthy Rolodex of names is more than a convenience; it is a survival tool. In turn, you should always be willing to lend an oar for your contacts when (not if) they need a favor you can deliver. You don't have to agree with other lobbyists—or even like them—to include them in your pool of resources. In that sense, lobbying is a shared enterprise; everyone has a stake in the process. Even some of those whom you are lobbying today will be lobbying you tomorrow. The more people in your network, the more valuable you are to the members you are trying to influence.

Following Up

The next day, follow up. First, write to the candidate, again reminding him or her of your issue. One form is as follows:

Dear Congressman Wiggles:

I enjoyed seeing you last night. As you know, the Flat Earth Society has always appreciated your support, and we are particularly grateful for your help in turning back H.R. 506. There have been several recent developments with regard to that bill that I would like to discuss with you at your convenience.

Thank you again for your help.

Sincerely,
Barton Strummer
Secretary
Flat Earth Society, Local 6

Next, write—or better yet call—the staffers you met at the reception. Remind them of the appointment you set up with the candidate and ask them to arrange a convenient time for the meeting. Stress that you would like to see them first and follow the procedures outlined in chapter 11.

Write a short, polite note to all the other people you met at the fundraiser. It's only for their files and to reestablish you in their memory. Keep a careful record of the fundraisers you have attended, just as you do for political contributions. This data will be useful in the future. One trick is to mark every business card you receive with the date and circumstances of your meeting. Record this information in your Rolodex.

Fundraisers are generally regarded as a necessary evil by candidates. These events expose them to all sorts of people they would rather not see, but it's not easy to refuse to talk to someone who has spent one hundred dollars for five minutes. Lobbyists should use that five minutes—or even one minute—to their greatest advantage. Candidates love contributors who are neither seen nor heard from, but you must be both.

14
GIMMICKS

"You can fool too many of the people too much of the time."

—James Thurber

Given the hundreds of special interest groups in Washington, it is sometimes difficult to be noticed. This is particularly true of smaller organizations. Sometimes, a citizen lobby resorts to unconventional methods merely to get some attention from the press or some public notoriety. Since reasoned, temperate debate neither sells newspapers nor attracts viewers to the six o'clock news, gimmicks may be one of the only ways to spark the media interest you feel you deserve. If you go this route, however, you should be sure the stunt you choose does not detract from your basic objective. The medium, in other words, cannot overwhelm the message.

Before you resort to a gimmick to promote your cause, consider the following factors:

Keep It Relevant to Your Issue

Mere grandstanding will not convey the message you want, however clever your stunt. One of the best gimmicks was staged by the right-to-life forces who deluged Capitol Hill with thousands of roses, each symbolizing an aborted fetus. This was both dramatic and relevant to the issue. Whoever thought of it was very media savvy.

Don't Be Disruptive

Although the American Agriculture Movement's "tractor-cade" to Washington was certainly relevant to its issue (low commodity prices), the disruption caused by hundreds of tractors destroying the Mall angered so many people that the farmers probably defeated their own purpose. A peaceful, even humorous, gimmick is much more likely to be favorably covered by the media.

Be careful to avoid less obvious forms of disruption as well. A few years ago in Florida, a doctor's group sent toy petri dishes to lawmakers' offices to draw attention to high malpractice insurance rates, but the gimmick caused a bioterrorism scare that instigated a police investigation.

Be Visible

Your gimmick is basically a publicity stunt, and to be picked up on the evening news, it must be visual. For example, mere complaints about rats in public housing projects are rarely enough to attract the broadcast media, but you might succeed in dramatizing the issue if you mount a full cage of rats on the top of a SUV and drive it down Pennsylvania Avenue. (This stunt was once successfully attempted in Washington, though some would suggest that the promoters went a little far in threatening to let loose thousands of rats in federal offices and residential areas if their demands were not met.)

Gimmicks sent through the mail rarely attract the kind of publicity you want—although they may get some attention on Capitol Hill, specifically from the Capitol Police. Sending packages through the mail to congressional offices is not recommended. Current security concerns may result in your mailing being delayed or even destroyed.

Contact the Press

No matter how clever, how relevant to your cause, or how visible, your gimmick will do you little good unless it is actually picked up by the media. Before you stage any stunt, be sure to alert the local news sources, particularly the television and radio stations. In Washington you should contact the news directors of the following stations:

Television

WUSA-TV (CBS)
4100 Wisconsin Avenue NW
Washington, DC 20016
(202) 895-5999
www.wusatv9.com

WRC-TV (NBC)
4001 Nebraska Avenue NW

Washington, DC 20016
(202) 885-4000
www.nbc4.com

WJLA-TV (ABC)
1100 Wilson Boulevard
Arlington, VA 22209
(702) 236-9552
www.wjla.com

WTTG-TV (FOX)
5151 Wisconsin Avenue NW
Washington, DC 20016
(202) 244-5151
www.myfoxdc.com

WDCW-TV (CW)
2121 Wisconsin Avenue NW, Suite 350
Washington, DC 20007
(202) 965-5050
http://thecwdc.trb.com

WETA-TV (PBS)
2775 South Quincy Street
Arlington, VA 22206
(703) 998-2600
www.weta.org/tv

Radio

WTOP
3400 Idaho Avenue NW
Washington, DC 20016
(202) 895-5000
www.wtop.com

WMAL
4400 Jennifer Street NW
Washington, DC 20015
(202) 686-3100
www.wmal.com

WAMU (PBS)
4000 Brandywine Street NW
Washington, DC 20016
(202) 885-1200
www.wamu.org

WFED (Federal News Radio)
3400 Idaho Avenue NW
Washington, DC 20016
(202) 895-5086
www.federalnewsradio.com

WPFW (Pacifica Radio)
2390 Champlain Street NW
Washington, DC 20009
(202) 588-0999
www.wpfw.org

WMET
8121 Georgia Avenue, Suite 806
Silver Spring, MD 20910
(866) 369-1160
www.wmet1160.com

Keep It Cheap

Your gimmick is more likely to be effective if you stress grassroots participation than if you go the route of costly extravaganzas. Use your imagination instead of your checkbook.

Successful Gimmicks

Although you must gear your gimmick to your particular issue, the following are a few examples of successful gimmicks that conform to the rules outlined above.

The National Chicken Council (formerly the National Broiler Council) represents the nation's chicken producers. For years, they staged a "chicken dog feast" in the courtyards of the Senate and House office buildings to acquaint congressional staffs with chicken-meat hot dogs. The issue being promoted by the council was that chicken dogs taste similar, if not identical, to regular beef or pork hot dogs and that producers should not be required to label these products "artificial hot dogs." These chicken dog feasts were usually held at about five o'clock on Friday afternoons during the summertime; the drawing card was not the hot dogs themselves, but the free beer that accompanied them. Nevertheless, the chicken dog issue became a cause celebre and the National Broiler Council's campaign ultimately succeeded. The total cost of the chicken dog feasts probably did not exceed a few thousand dollars per year, but they were known throughout Washington as one of the most ingenious and successful lobbying campaigns in recent memory.

Each year the Can Manufacturers Institute distributes beautiful Christmas tree ornaments fashioned from cleverly reshaped tin cans. There is hardly a member of Congress or congressional staff member in town who does not have one of these on his or her Christmas tree. Although CMI is not attempting to promote a specific bill, everyone in Washington recognizes the CMI ornaments and remembers the organization for at least one month a year.

Similarly, the Ferrous Scrap Consumers Coalition distributed paperweights made of steel scrap and emblazoned with the message that this commodity was one of America's vanishing resources. Thousands were given away on the Hill at a nominal cost to the steel companies.

The Distilled Spirits Council of the United States (DISCUS) not only sent samples of its products around the Hill at various times of the year, but also provided congressional offices with posters and other advertising materials to distribute to members' constituencies urging responsibility in alcohol use. The members often sent these to high schools in their states or districts, for incalculable political benefits all at little cost to DISCUS.

The electric utilities have distributed free light bulbs to the Hill. Although the total cost of this project was probably significant, the lobby certainly did not violate any gift restrictions since each recipient received only one or two.

Various conservation groups visited the Hill with enormous displays of leghold traps to publicize their view that such devices are cruel to animals. The displays were widely covered by the media and resulted in federal legislation restricting the use of such devices.

A fifty-five-gallon drum of polluted river water was brought to Washington by an environmentalist group that threatened to dump it into the Potomac as a media stunt if stricter water pollution control guidelines were not adopted. It is not known what happened to the polluted water, but the desired environmental legislation was adopted.

These are only some of the ideas others have come up with to publicize their programs. Undoubtedly, you can think of even more effective stunts.

15

THE HILL BLITZ

"I once said cynically of a politician, 'He'll double-cross that bridge when he comes to it.'"

—Oscar Levant

What Is a Blitz?

In the last two decades, the Hill blitz has evolved into something approaching an art form. As its name implies, it is a swift and concentrated strategic attack on Capitol Hill. Over the course of two to three days, you will employ all available resources, from constituent contacts to favors owed by congressional offices, to express your organization's views in the halls of the Congress. A blitz is the most formidable short-term pressure you can put on members of Congress and the most efficient means of consolidating your resources, and it should be included in every lobbying campaign.

The blitz can be a frustrating experience, and your own presence of mind will be severely tried during its planning stage. The major challenge of a Hill blitz is not substantive but procedural. To be successful, a blitz must be planned weeks or even months in advance; you must gather the most senior representatives of your cause in Washington at the same time. If you spread the blitz out over a week or two for the sake of your representatives' schedules, its effectiveness—for both your members and the Hill—would be dissipated.

Preparation and Appointments

As a rule, you should budget at least three weeks to adequately prepare even a modest blitz of 20 or so participants. The more of your supporters you have coming to Washington, the more time you should allow yourself.

Your administrative concerns will be identical in most respects to those involved in planning a demonstration (see chapter 7). The distinction between a demonstration, a loose amalgam of people chanting in the streets, and a blitz is your focus on the Hill. Before you make a single telephone call to arrange an appointment, you must prepare a thorough analysis of crucial congressmen and senators on the basis of constituent relations, interest in your issue, committee assignments, and past support. You should have already prepared your list of target members, together with their backgrounds, in your resource book and action plan (see chapters 3 and 4).

The first priority in setting up blitz appointments is constituent relations. A participant in the blitz from a member's state or district should always be given precedence in meeting his or her representative. Call the office of each member for whom you will have a constituent participating in the blitz. Tell the personal secretary the nature of your issue and that a constituent of the member will be in Washington a few weeks hence. Request a meeting on a particular day during the period of the blitz, and be sure to get two or three alternate times when the member would be able to meet with your people. Tell the secretary that you will call to reconfirm one of the times within a few days. Obviously, the reason you have requested alternate dates is that your calendar will be filled with conflicts and you want to be able to shift meeting times around.

After you have completed your constituent-related calls, contact the congressional offices that have given you the greatest support. Even though it may appear that you are lobbying the converted, you cannot afford to alienate your friends by ignoring them. They should at least be given the courtesy of a visit and kept informed of your efforts. Finally, you should contact committee and subcommittee chairmen and any other members of Congress who may directly impact your cause. The actual number of offices you contact will, of course, depend on the number of participants in your blitz, their constituent relations, and the amount of time your participants are prepared to spend in Washington.

After you have completed all your preliminary calls, divide the participants in your blitz into three- or four-person teams. Assign team leaders, who will be responsible for making sure all appointments are kept, protocol is observed, and facts are presented in the way you intend. The team leaders should be constituent blitz participants, and if possible each team should contain constituents from several different districts. If two or more organizations are participating in the blitz, it is generally best not to include members of different groups on the same teams unless the organizations have a very close and long-standing working relationship. Mixing team members is an invitation to personal and institutional rivalries that can detract from your message.

Once you have designated your teams, you should schedule them for times when the members of Congress are available, placing the highest priority on constituent relations. Even though few interviews will take more than fifteen to twenty minutes, each team should be assigned to visit no more than six congressional offices in a given day. The reason for this modest number of visits is logistical—even though you will have made appointments, delays are inevitable. You should also allow plenty of time—at least fifteen to twenty minutes—for walking from one congressional office to the next, especially if your blitz participants are unfamiliar with the Hill, or a team has to go from the House to the Senate side to visit the members of a constituent's congressional delegation. Make a master calendar of all teams' appointments, cross-indexed by member of Congress, team, and time. You, as the coordinator, must know where every team will be at all times.

If there are an inordinately large number of blitz participants from a single state or district, you may want to schedule a joint meeting of several teams with the member. If you do so, be sure to tell the member's secretary so that accommodations can be made. Most members' offices will only comfortably accommodate six or seven people.

After you have completed your calendar, call back each of the congressional offices and confirm your appointments. Inevitably, between the first time you called and the time you confirm the appointments there will have been changes in the member's calendar. Even with a modest-sized list, you will have to make scores of telephone calls and rework your schedule several times before it is complete.

Once your calendar is in its final form, you should prepare separate versions for each team. A sample calendar for a team might be arranged as follows:

Flat Earth Society—Congressional Contact Team Number Five

Mary Butrum, Team Leader, Redlands, Calif.
David Hawkins, Fairfield, Conn.
Sara Knowles, Lancaster, Pa.

Monday, September 24

8:00 A.M.: breakfast for all team members
Washington Hilton Hotel

9:30 A.M.: depart for Capitol Hill

10:00 A.M.: Congresswoman Helen Blanchard (D-PA)
3240 Rayburn House Office Building
Telephone: 555-0113
Staff Contact: Millie Tightfist

10:45 A.M.: Congressman James Crossman (R-CA)
320 Cannon House Office Building
Telephone: 555-0116
Staff Contact: Melvin Scrumpus

11:20 A.M.: Congressman Lupis Wolf (D-CT)
3270 Rayburn House Office Building
Telephone: 555-0104
Staff Contact: Bill Weevel

12:10 P.M.: lunch with staff of House Education Subcommittee
(Lorna Doone, Betty Crocker, Frank Bertolli)
209½ Restaurant
209½ Pennsylvania Avenue SE
Reservations in name of Mary Butrum

1:45 P.M.: Senator Calvin Hoover (R-PA)
421 Dirksen Senate Office Building
Telephone: 555-0163
Staff Contact: Ronald Kennedy

2:30 P.M.: Senator Abraham Arthur (I-PA)
3240 Russell Senate Office Building
Telephone: 555-0140
Staff Contact: George Madison

4:00 P.M.: Senator James Grant (R-TN)
415 Dirksen Senate Office Building
Telephone: 555-0156
Staff Contact: Roosevelt McKinley

5:30 P.M.: cocktail reception for members and congressional staff
Gold Room, Rayburn House Office Building

Tuesday, September 25

8:00 A.M.: breakfast for all team members
Washington Hilton Hotel

9:30 A.M.: depart for Capitol Hill

10:15 A.M.: Congressman J. D. "Whimpie" Burke (D-CA)
1421 Longworth House Office Building
Telephone: 555-0166
Staff Contact: Benjamin Dover

11:00 A.M.: *Congresswoman Stella Schnellzug (R-TN)*
3160 Longworth House Office Building
Telephone: 555-0146
Staff Contact: Harry David

12:15 P.M.: *lunch with members of Senate Education Committee*
(Plato Brown, Mauna Lowa)
The Man in the Green Hat Restaurant
301 Massachusetts Avenue NE
Reservations in name of Mary Butrum

2:00 P.M.: *depart Reagan National Airport*

Each team member will be given a copy of the schedule, along with the following items:

- short biographies of each member of Congress with whom they have an appointment
- summary sheets to leave with each congressional office
- interview sheets

The interview sheets are to be filled out by each team member after each congressional visit. They describe in detail the nature of the meeting and any commitments made by the congressman or senator to the group. Also included should be each team member's personal reactions to the interview—whether it went smoothly, whether the member was hostile or friendly, whether he or she seemed to be aware of the issue. Finally, each team member should indicate what questions were asked by the member or the member's staff. You will follow up on them later.

Coordination

There has never been a Hill blitz in which something did not go wrong— appointments canceled, participants lost, meetings missed, or lawmakers insulted. During the blitz, your place is not on Capitol Hill, but in a central location with a telephone. If possible, you should have an aide assigned to making spot checks on the Hill to see that everything is going as planned. There will, however, be dozens of questions that require your immediate attention; you must be reachable quickly.

In addition, you must be sure the lines of authority for managing the blitz are clearly drawn; it would be an unusual organization that did not have five or six individuals who will never be satisfied with their schedules and who will want to depart from their assigned interviews. When multiple organizations are involved, coordination among the various groups is essential; you cannot afford to have six different sets of instructions for your teams. You should have a single coordinator for the entire blitz who has been agreed upon in advance by all participating groups.

The coordinator will also be responsible for making luncheon plans and in some cases dinner reservations for teams meeting with member of Congress, and restructuring team membership as required by unforeseen events. The role is time-consuming and difficult, but it is also critical to a successful effort.

The Meeting

The actual meetings of your teams with the senators and congressmen should follow the procedures outlined in chapter 11. During a blitz, however, you will not be present at the actual interviews; the team leaders will act as your surrogates. It is therefore important that they be fully briefed on your entire lobbying effort.

It is desirable to have the team leaders meet with you just prior to the blitz. At this meeting, you will describe the logistics of the event, the procedures to be followed in the congressional meetings, and the strategy and tactics of your lobbying campaign. Team leaders should be provided with a resource book (see chapter 3). As noted previously, this book should be held in confidence and should not be distributed to all team members, but the team leaders should be given an opportunity to thoroughly familiarize themselves with the issues, statistics, and facts contained in it before they are unleashed on the Hill. In addition, review with them the procedures outlined in chapter 11 and try to anticipate all questions that may arise on the Hill. Emphasize to the team leaders the importance of maintaining a schedule and limiting their interviews with members of Congress to fifteen or twenty minutes.

Finally, stress the importance of filling out the interview sheets. It will be the team leader's responsibility to collect them from the team and give them to you at the end of each day of the blitz. You should review the first day's interview sheets immediately to see if any team received too many obvious questions, which may be an indication that your team leader was not fully briefed. Correcting this problem quickly will ensure that for the rest of the blitz, the team will be able to answer these questions on the spot and you will not have to follow up later. It is always most effective if it appears that your adherents are knowledgeable—if they don't have to go back to headquarters for answers to the simplest questions.

Several trade associations train team leaders by staging mock congressional meetings and rehearsing the methodology to be employed. This is an extremely effective method of training your troops and should be done no more than twenty-four hours in advance of your actual blitz.

Follow-Up

Perhaps the most important part of your Hill blitz is following up on the contacts you have made. First, review all the interview sheets prepared by your team members. First priority should go to answering questions posed by members of Congress or their staffs. If the nature of the question implies a degree of urgency (e.g., how your organization stands on a bill pending on the floor of the House), you should follow up with a telephone call to the appropriate staff member of the congressman or senator asking the question. In most cases, questions will not be so urgent as to demand telephone follow-up. They should, however, be promptly answered in writing.

You should also write to every congressman, senator, and staff member who attended the meetings, thanking them for their courtesy in receiving your delegation. This can be a form letter, but you should personalize it if you know the individual to whom you're writing, or if you're writing to a staffer who was instrumental in helping you arrange the meeting.

Finally, you should have each team member write personal letters to all the individuals they met during the blitz. These letters should be written within one week after the blitz and you should request that copies of them be sent to you for your files.

Based on the information collected during the blitz, you should be able to make a relatively accurate estimate of your supporters and to analyze your chances of success. Add this information to your resource book, particularly if members of Congress have made commitments to your team regarding their opposition, support, or neutrality on your issue.

16

WHAT IF THINGS
GO WRONG?

"Nothing is so admirable in politics as a short memory."

—John Kenneth Galbraith

In even the most carefully prepared lobbying campaign, many things will go wrong. Appointments will be missed, decimal points dropped in your statistical tables, key members of Congress inadvertently left off invitation lists, or important staffers insulted. Since these slipups are virtually inevitable, it is best to prepare for them before they occur.

Errors of Fact

Nothing is more valuable to a lobbyist than his or her credibility. Although members of Congress and their staffs know you are expressing a point of view and take that into consideration when they decide how to act on your issue, they have a right to expect that the objective information you supply—e.g., statistics, names, dates—will be complete and accurate. Accuracy is particularly important for congressional offices that support your position. If your allies rely on incorrect information you have supplied them, the consequences may be embarrassing and even devastating. This is not to say you shouldn't emphasize facts that enhance your position, but withholding essential information or inventing numbers must be absolutely forbidden.

Additional Information

During the course of any lobbying effort, you will certainly be asked to provide additional information. There is a difference, however, between simply not having information at hand and actively withholding information. If a congressional office asks you to provide additional data, promise to do so as soon as possible—and then follow up. If you cannot locate the information requested, contact the person who made the inquiry and say so. Do not leave the impression that you have ignored the request—or, worse yet, that you are withholding bad news.

Sources

Aside from the ethics of supplying correct information, there is the practical side: fact-checking. Time is well spent proofreading every document you send to the Hill for typographical errors and misstatements of fact. It is also useful if you can supply footnotes or otherwise indicate the source of your information in all documents sent to the Hill. The most credible sources are reports from government agencies; information and numbers supplied by your own group are sometimes regarded as being tainted by self-interest.

If you have any reason to believe that the factual data may not present the entire picture or may give an incorrect impression, it is always best to qualify the information with footnotes or other explanations. Sometimes, for example, government statistics themselves are in error, or at least misleading. If your opponents are using such information to attack your position, it is best to find a third-party source that directly questions the accuracy of the government's data. If it is merely your word against that of the government, you will usually lose.

Statistics

Statistics can be twisted in remarkable ways to demonstrate your point of view. For example, a study might show a series of very small numerical increases over a period of months or years, but they might represent significant *percentage* increases, in which case you would report the percentages. Conversely, a large numerical increase might not result in a significant percentage increase, in which case you would report the raw numbers instead.

Consider the following charts:

Chart 1

Instances of Ships Falling Off the Edge of the World

1995	13
1996	15
1997	20
1998	25
1999	30
2000	35

(Source: *Flat Earth Society Digest*)

Chart 2

Unexplained Losses of Ships

1995	250
1996	265
1997	271
1998	282
1999	286
2000	291

(Source: *Lloyd's of Boston*)

Between 1995 and 2000, the figures shown in chart 1 increase by over 169 percent, but the figures in chart 2 increase by only about 16 percent. In presenting your statistics, you would use the percentage figure from chart 1 and the raw numbers from chart 2, as in the following text:

According to several studies, including the famous Lloyds of Boston *Annual Survey of Shipping Losses*, ships have been disappearing at an alarming rate. In 2000 alone, Lloyds reported 291 such disasters. Many of these losses are the result of ships falling off the edge of the world. Between 1995 and 2000, such calamities have increased by over 169 percent.

There are much more sophisticated methods of presenting statistics, including use of semilog graphs, econometric modeling, and least-square trend lines. You should experiment with various methods to find the one best suited to enhancing your position. These methods are not misstatements of fact, but merely ways to present your case in the best possible light. It is important, however, to indicate to the congressional offices the methodology you used to arrive at your statistical conclusions.

If, no matter how you twist and bend them, the statistics simply do not support your position, resist the temptation to invent numbers or manipulate them dishonestly. An attempt to do so will almost always be counterproductive. Remember, your opponents—if they're any good at all—will be scrutinizing your propaganda. If they discover an obvious distortion, the credibility of your entire position will be jeopardized, especially if it appears that you have consciously attempted to deceive members of Congress and their staffs.

Things Go Wrong

You've decided to play it straight. You've reviewed the numbers and stressed those that most enhance your position. You've double-checked them for errors.

Nothing can go wrong, but the computer gremlins have it in for you this week and all the decimal points in your statistics have been moved one figure to the left. Documents have already been sent to 117 congressional offices, and speech writers, relying on the data you supplied, are cranking out blistering commentary on your behalf. Now you discover the error.

The first thing to do is to immediately reproof the entire document. Other mistakes may have crept in and it is best to correct all errors at one time. Once you are satisfied that all errors have been caught, make a prioritized list of persons who should know about it. If you are aware of certain congressional offices that are preparing speeches, newsletters, or any other documents, don't write— call. In most cases the person to contact will be the legislative assistant who handles your issue. Tell the LA of the error or errors and provide the correct information. In addition, tell him or her that you will be sending an errata sheet with corrected information immediately.

Next, pull out your list of those who received the incorrect information and send them all an errata sheet. If possible, the sheet should be identical to the page on which the errors appeared in the original document. It can be a photocopy of the page with the correct numbers inserted. If this is not possible because of the format of the original document, a small paper slip should be sent with the correct information. If you sent the original document as an e-mail attachment, prepare a new attachment with a new date clearly marked within the document itself, in the file name, and in the subject line of the e-mail. The errata slip or sheet should be accompanied by a short, straightforward note. The format might be as follows:

Errata

The Flat Earth Society publication Square Corners dated July 9, 2007, contained an error on page 26. A new page 26 with the correct information is attached. Please discard the original page 26 and insert the attached.

The Flat Earth Society regrets the error.

The important thing about correcting errors is that you do it promptly and that you supply accurate information at the time you make the correction. Correcting simple errors of fact should almost always be done—but don't make a big deal of it. You should flag such errors with the degree of urgency warranted by the nature of the mistake. Typographical errors may be ignored if they do not change the meaning of your statements, but statistical errors should be corrected as soon as possible.

A more difficult situation is an oral or written misstatement of fact by a member of your group to a congressional or administrative office. Often, you will not discover such misstatements until days or even weeks have passed. When you realize what has happened, immediately get in touch with the person who conveyed the misinformation. Discuss the matter with that individual and have him or her contact the persons to whom the incorrect information was communicated. It is embarrassing for anyone to have to do this, but the damage will be far greater if you are forced to publicly contradict your own member. If for any reason your member refuses, or is unable to correct the error, you should do so yourself in as low-key a manner as possible. Do not merely let the matter rest.

Perhaps the most difficult and sensitive situation of all is when a member of Congress supporting your position misstates essential facts. This is not a rare occurrence; the *Congressional Record* is replete with errors. These errors can be used both offensively and defensively. You should carefully review all public statements by your opponents and, when you discover an error, use it to your advantage. The best way to do so is to photocopy the offending document, underline the erroneous statements or statistics in red, and prepare a short rebuttal piece with accurate statistics. It helps if your rejoinder can be footnoted with unimpeachable sources. The rebuttal piece should then be distributed to all of your allies and, if possible, inserted into the *Congressional Record*. This technique is most useful where major errors of fact are apparent. Do not submit a rebuttal to an extremely minor error, as it will make you appear to be a nitpicker.

When your own side makes an error, it is generally best to approach the appropriate legislative assistant first. You should do this as soon as you discover the error and, you hope, before the other side has noticed it. You should follow the legislative assistant's advice on how to correct the misstatement. Some congressional offices will put a correction in the "Extension of Remarks" of the *Congressional Record* immediately, others might choose to explain the discrepancy away through deft use of polemics, and still others might ignore it altogether. Even if you expect them to choose the latter course, it is important that you at least notify the congressional office of the mistake. It is unlikely they will repeat the error. If they do, you might consider going to the administrative assistant. These types of errors reflect poorly on the congressman or senator's credibility, and that is a political concern and thus the AA's domain.

Changed Circumstances

During the course of any lobbying campaign, numbers, names, and even the facts themselves will change. Change is inevitable and everyone in Washington recognizes that statistics and other factual bases for your claims may become less—

or more—reliable as time goes on. About the only way to really go wrong, given the dynamics of the Washington system, is to fail to acknowledge the ephemeral nature of your facts. No one will raise an eyebrow if you change numbers based upon better, more recent information, but you will arouse suspicion if you fail to update your data.

These changes, however, can as often work against you as for you. For example, if you're dealing with a situation in which monthly statistics are a major factor, aberrations in the marketplace can destroy your best arguments almost overnight. As discussed previously, there are ways to present your statistics that, although still accurate, will present a better slant on your position. Consider the following:

Number of Flat Earth Society Members

2002	200
2003	300
2004	650
2005	1,400
2006	912

The above chart shows a decline in the membership of your organization in the most recent year, and this is likely to raise eyebrows on Capitol Hill. One way to handle this problem is to eliminate the chart entirely and include references to membership in the text of your paper. A reworking of the information included in the chart might read as follows: "The Flat Earth Society continues to grow at a remarkable pace. In 2002 it had only 200 members. By 2006, membership stood at 912, an increase of over 400 percent." This is about as close as you should ever come to "reworking" information; this technique obviously fails to mention that there was an actual decline in 2006, but it does not raise the suspicion that you have failed to update your numbers.

Insults and Breaches of Protocol

Although Washington is often portrayed as a city of impassioned rhetoric, more pointed insults are probably traded on loading docks in Brooklyn than in the U.S. Senate. The Senate is the lair of wordsmiths. Insults are carefully crafted and tenderly slipped between opponents' ribs, sometimes without their knowledge. Senator Everett Dirksen was fond of retelling the following story about insults on Capitol Hill:

> If one of your opponents starts out a speech on the floor by saying, "My colleague, the senator from Illinois, is mistaken," then you don't have to worry too

much. If he starts out his speech with, "My esteemed colleague, the distinguished senator from the great state of Illinois . . .," then you'd better listen. And if he prefaces his remarks by saying, "My great and dear friend, the distinguished and esteemed senator from the great state of Illinois, the land of Lincoln . . . ," then you'd better not turn your back.

Although it is possible that you will be insulted during the course of a lobbying campaign, it will probably be artfully done. The rules about how to react are simple: don't.

It is different, however, when you or, more likely, one of your supporters or members insults a member of Congress or congressional staffer. This usually happens when lobbyists reach their frustration limit with the bureaucracy, particularly when out-of-town lobbyists visit numerous congressional offices and encounter only inertia. Many people outside the Beltway tend to regard Washington not just as another city, but also as a foreign country populated by a peculiar race of drones. It can become frustrating after you've visited fifteen congressional offices and have received nothing but polite assurances from bland young men and women that they will "look into it." A typical reaction at the end of a Hill blitz is for one of your members to look at the twenty-three-year-old who holds the destiny of your issue in his or her hands and to say something like, "You bastard, have you been listening to what I've been telling you? The whole world's falling apart and you're just sitting there like a clam in gumbo." Hardly a day passes on the Hill when someone doesn't offer to throw a junior legislative assistant out a fifth-floor window of the Rayburn Building. Perhaps that's why the Congress needs so many police officers (there are three capitol cops for every member of Congress).

Although such an outburst might make the speaker feel a little less frustrated, it's unlikely to do much for your group's image as moderate, thoughtful, and objective. Screaming matches tend to reflect an image of extremism and can severely injure your chances of success in both the short and the long term. Besides, almost no one on Capitol Hill will be impressed or intimidated by threats or curses.

If such an outburst does occur, however, you should immediately separate the curser from the cursee. Politely but firmly suggest to the member of your group that you think there is little more that can be accomplished and declare the interview terminated. In certain situations this may be difficult to do; your colleague probably won't express much goodwill for you at the time. As soon as possible, go back to the congressional office to salve the wounds. Whether or not you should apologize depends on the circumstances. Don't wear sackcloth and ashes for minor indiscretions, but don't be afraid to express your sincere regrets if you or your group committed a major gaffe.

A far more common form of insult in Washington is the "bruised ego" syndrome. Members of Congress tend to have an inflated sense of their own worth. This condition is highly contagious and usually affects staff members early in their tenure. Whether their fond self-image is justified is of little consequence; it is not your responsibility to inform them of their true worth. Merely recognize the way things are in Washington and learn how to deal with the situation. Remember, you're not just lobbying for your own personal satisfaction; your goal is to change the course of legislative events in the country. You can't effectively accomplish this if you don't learn to live with the realities of the world.

The most frequent manner in which tender egos are bruised is not by malfeasance, but by nonfeasance. Legislative assistants are often furious if they are ignored or, worse yet, if a lobbyist goes over their head to an administrative assistant or the actual member of Congress. Some members are highly sensitive to being ignored on issues about which they feel particularly knowledgeable. Ignoring such people can be almost as bad as insulting them to their face. Even if they can't do you much good, and including them in your campaign will require a great deal more effort on your part, leaving them out of your lobbying plans can be very dangerous. General rules to follow in this regard are

+ Always keep the legislative assistant of the congressional offices you are in contact with informed of your program and any meetings you have had with his or her superiors.

+ Include press aides in your rounds if any part of your program consists of press releases by the member's office or using the member's name.

+ Never refer to a member of Congress by first name unless you are extremely good friends. Although few congressmen or senators will directly contradict you, most enjoy being referred to as "Senator," "Congressman," or "Congresswoman." It is better to be invited to use first names than to be resented for not using the honorific.

+ Get a sense of the degree of formality of a congressional office by seeing how the staff members themselves interact. In some offices three-piece suits are worn and secretaries refer to AAs and LAs as "Mr." or "Ms." In others, where open-neck shirts and sunglasses predominate, the only thing you'll hear are nicknames. Try to adjust your approach to the formality of the office, and be slightly more formal than they are.

+Never condescend to anyone in a congressional office, no matter how young or inexperienced a person may appear. Entire lobbying campaigns have been blown by the president of a trade association referring to a secretary as "little girl" or to an African American LA as "you people."

+Always be sure the chairmen of the subcommittee and full committee that are considering your issue are aware of your existence and what you are attempting to do, even if they are likely to oppose you. This is not to suggest that you must include them in the specifics of every action you intend to take, only that chairmen are highly sensitive about knowing what is going on in their own committees. They can be obstinate if they are left in the dark about something. It's not necessary for you to speak directly to the chairman, but the chairman's staff should receive at least a cursory briefing.

+Be very judicious in criticizing members of congressional staffs to any other Hill staffers. As large as it is, the Hill staff still regards itself as a family. You may be unaware of a personal relationship that exists between the person you are speaking to and the person you are criticizing.

17

DO YOU NEED A
PROFESSIONAL?

"Politics is not a science . . . but an art."

—Otto von Bismarck

What a Professional Lobbyist Can and Can't Do

If you follow the guidelines in this book, you should, with a little practice, have
no difficulty in organizing your own lobbying campaign. An important factor
that must be dealt with, however, is the time investment required to adequately
administer such an effort. A professional's dedicated involvement can help you
cope with the schedule demands. A professional can also provide experience in
general legislative matters and organizational ability. Never hire an outside lobbyist with the expectation that he or she can carry the ball for you or buy influence. A professional will only be a spokesperson for your cause; you and your
members must still provide the clout necessary for him or her to present a credible case.

In that respect, hiring a lobbyist is somewhat different from retaining a
lawyer. You have a right to expect that lawyers know considerably more than you
do about the intricacies of the law, and after you have told them all the facts in
your particular case, you should usually trust their judgment on how a legal proceeding should be handled. In other words, you put yourself and your case in
their hands. Although this is true to a certain extent with professional lobbyists,
you should feel much more comfortable helping to run your own lobbying campaign than you would advising counsel on how best to present a case in court.
Since lobbyists do not necessarily have any specialized training or experience
and few colleges offer courses on how to lobby (no degree has ever been awarded

in this profession), it is possible you will know as much about lobbying as the professional does. You will almost certainly know more about your particular issue than any lobbyist you retain, and it will be up to you to educate him or her regarding the facts and politics of the cause.

Over the years, dozens of books have been written and hundreds of stories told about Washington miracle workers who could turn around the course of legislative events on behalf of a client with one telephone call. Such stories tend to perpetuate the myth of the omniscient lobbyist with a monopoly on influence peddling and with whom no one could seriously hope to compete. Some of these stories are apocryphal; others are so exceptional as to demonstrate the truth of the rule that hard work, not personal influence, is the most important factor in a successful lobbying campaign.

This is not to suggest that a lifetime of building contacts on the Hill and in the administrative agencies will not be rewarding. Personal relationships built upon years of trust can provide access and credibility for an experienced lobbyist that may not come readily to the neophyte. Any good professional lobbyist will carefully nurture such personal relationships and use them sparingly. It is important to distinguish, however, between access and action. An "old Washington hand" may be able to walk into a congressman or senator's office and greet the member by his first name, but although this talent is impressive and unquestionably useful, few successful lobbying campaigns start or end there. In short, few if any professional lobbyists have a significant degree of personal political power. They can, however, help maximize the power you have through their contacts and credibility, built up over the years.

Thus, when you decide whether or not you need a professional, look first to your own ability to devote the necessary time to the lobbying campaign. Next, check your finances to determine whether you can afford a professional's fees. Finally, recognize in advance that professional lobbyists are not shamans. They cannot work miracles for you and will borrow your clout to make your case on the Hill.

How Much Will It Cost?

Asking how much a professional lobbyist will cost is like asking how much a car costs—it depends on what you want, a stripped-down compact or a fully loaded Mercedes. Between these extremes, however, there is a broad spectrum in which cost and quality are not necessarily related. There are as many Edsels in the lobbying field as in any other area; a six-figure fee does not guarantee Rolls-Royce quality.

The two basic methods of charging lobbying clients are a flat fee on one hand, and a retainer and an hourly rate on the other. Some professionals, especially independent lobbying consultants, may insist upon a flat fee; others, particularly lawyers, may agree to an hourly rate. When you first retain a professional lobbyist, it is almost always to your advantage to request an hourly charge. A flat fee, particularly if it includes expenses, is an open invitation to lobbyists to cut costs so they can maximize their own profits. Often, a flat fee will also encourage a lobbyist to spend as little time as possible on your project. Although some flat-fee proponents argue that this system could as easily work to the advantage of a client who succeeds in negotiating a low flat fee and then demands extensive services, this scenario rarely happens.

A flat-fee arrangement does have the advantage of predictability, thus simplifying the drawing up of a lobbying budget, which is difficult until you have a sense of what you can expect from a lobbyist and at what price. It is usually best if you start on an hourly basis and graduate to a fixed-fee formula.

How to Choose a Professional Lobbyist

You have decided that neither you nor anyone in your group can dedicate the time necessary to administer a lobbying campaign in Washington. You have met with your members and agreed to retain a professional to assist you, recognizing that your group will be working with whomever you select on a regular basis and that you're not merely turning over the problem to him or her. How do you go about finding someone who meets both your needs and your budget? Lobbyists are not listed under their own heading in the Yellow Pages, and even the reference books cited in chapter 19 (e.g., *Washington Representatives*) will be of little use to you in compiling a list of potential candidates. This is odd considering that thousands of people in Washington would be eager to undertake the responsibility of representing your cause.

There are three types of organizations in Washington that regularly represent and lobby for special interest groups: law firms, public relations agencies, and specialized lobbying firms. Each of them has its own advantages and drawbacks, and you may decide to retain more than one to address different needs.

Law Firms

There are more than thirty-five thousand lawyers in Washington; they are listed in the Yellow Pages, as well as in such legal directories as Martindale-Hubbell, found at www.martindale.com. Although the legal directories provide somewhat greater detail than mere listings in the Yellow Pages, even the biographies contained in Martindale-Hubbell do not provide a reasonable basis for selecting a law firm and can be deceptive on important issues.

You should recognize that law firms in Washington serve a different function than firms anywhere else in the country. Many Washington firms have the attitude that if all else fails, get the law changed. They are less likely to recommend litigation than firms in cities more attuned to the traditional role of lawyers. A significant number of Washington lawyers have never appeared in court nor opened a law book in years. They know nothing more than the layman about such traditional legal issues as wills, divorces, taxes, or how to present a case to a jury. Their livelihood is strictly predicated on their knowledge of the Washington political system—which, some would say, has little to do with either law or justice.

Despite their lack of traditional legal skills, these lawyer-lobbyists can sometimes provide the best representation for private interest groups. In the first place, most of them are members of law firms that provide a wide range of both legal and extralegal services to their clients. When faced with legal questions with which they are unfamiliar, lawyer-lobbyists are able to avail themselves of expertise within their own organization. For example, if a lawyer-lobbyist is working on changes in a particular piece of legislation, he or she can call upon other more traditionally oriented attorneys in the firm to provide legal analyses of the way existing law has been interpreted by the courts. Many lawyer-lobbyists also claim their own legal specialization, a particular area of the law in which they are competent to analyze the technical aspects of a given problem. In many circumstances, these are invaluable advantages. Of all the available forms of third-party assistance, law firms offer the greatest variety of representation and in most cases can provide you with the service you need at a reasonable cost.

Law firms are by far the most common source for outside lobbying assistance. Consequently, a good starting point for selecting a law firm to represent your interests is to contact trade associations, unions, or other groups with interests and objectives similar to your own and ask them if they are represented by Washington counsel and how satisfied they are with the service they have received compared with the costs they have incurred. For each firm, secure the name of at least one attorney with whom they regularly dealt. It is a good idea to contact six or seven interest groups and compile a list of every firm mentioned. Do not drop a firm merely because you receive one bad report; often, an interest group will give a particular firm bad ratings because of political and personal considerations. It should also be emphasized that although you will generally retain a law firm to represent you, you will almost certainly not have contact with everyone there. One or a few people within the firm will be given responsibility for your affairs. While a firm may have a good (or bad) reputation for representing clients, you should withhold final judgment until you actually have an opportunity to meet the individuals with whom you would be working.

Once you have compiled your list of law firms, you should arrange with senior members of your group, or a committee selected for this purpose, to accompany you to Washington for interviews. It would be wise to bring at least two or three other people with you; their impressions may be different from yours. It is also advisable, when picking your selection committee, to choose the most hard-bitten, objective members; silver-tongued Washington lawyers can impress the gullible all too easily. This advice is the most likely to be ignored in this entire book. We all think we can take care of ourselves, but we're dealing with pros here.

Do not contact any law firm until you have arranged a convenient time for your own people to travel to the capital. If you and your people meet regularly, you may wish to have the candidates travel to you. This alternative is less desirable, because the lawyers may charge you a fee to attend an out-of-town meeting. Be sure you clarify this point before you invite them.

Once you have arranged a convenient time for your people to visit Washington, call the firms on your list. First, try to reach one of the attorneys mentioned in your conversations with the other interest groups. If that person is not there, ask to speak with one of his or her associates (in a law firm, "associate" means "junior attorney"). Explain who you are to the attorney with whom you speak and say that you would like to meet with him or her on a specific day. Most firms will be pleased to accommodate you—remember, you are the client and it is the firm's obligation to arrange its schedule around yours. If you have given adequate notice (at least ten days) and the firm seems reluctant to have anyone meet with you on the day you request, immediately strike it from your list.

It would be unreasonable to expect, of course, that the individual attorney with whom you originally spoke will, in every case, be able to meet with you at your convenience, since if a lawyer is any good at all, he or she will probably have other clients who demand similar attention. But it is important to select a firm that is professional enough to provide *someone* in authority who can meet with you at your convenience and who is adequately briefed on your needs. This usually means you will seek out firms with at least two or three attorneys. You need not, however, go to extremes. A firm with six or seven attorneys is often as fully capable of delivering top-quality service as one with hundreds. Size becomes important only to the extent that there is always someone available to you, quite literally on a twenty-four-hour basis. If a firm is unwilling or unable to even discuss matters with a potential new client, they may already be so overworked that they are not interested in representing you. You have a right to expect both courtesy and restrained enthusiasm from the outset.

You should count on an interview schedule of two to four firms per day. Start your schedule in the morning with a meeting of your own people at breakfast. All of them should be carefully briefed on what you're looking for and the schedule of events. The interviews that follow should be conducted in the offices of your prospective law firms. This will give you a chance to get a feel for the people with whom you will be working.

You may be invited to lunch during the interview process. This is a traditional Washington ploy, so do not be overly impressed. You should, however, allow the lawyer to pick up the check. If a firm is really eager to represent your group, the attorneys you are meeting with will usually pay the tab. If they don't, store that fact in the back of your mind and graciously accept the check yourself.

In each interview, you should be prepared to give the attorneys a general briefing on the nature of your work, as well as the statistical basis for your claims. One way to judge the enthusiasm of the firm for your cause is by the amount of background research, if any, they have done prior to your meeting. If they are diligent, they will have done at least some cursory research on your issue and should be able to listen intelligently. It would be a mistake, however, to expect them to have as thorough a knowledge of your problem as you have.

After you have described the pertinent issues, ask the attorneys how they would approach a lobbying campaign for your cause. Give them an opportunity to fully explain their methodology, then ask as many relevant questions as possible. Do not be reluctant to put them on the spot. Better that you discover their inadequacies now than later, after you have incurred thousands of dollars in fees. Try to be as cynical as courtesy will permit. Don't trust just your own judgment; rely on the cumulative impressions of the entire interview committee.

You should ask the attorneys about other lobbying efforts in which they have been involved and the people with whom they have dealt in groups similar to your own. The people and groups they mention, some of which may not be familiar to you, may have different impressions of the firm than those who originally referred you. You will want to follow up with them at the conclusion of your interview schedule.

The firm's lobbying history is also important because professional lobbyists are often known for having a particular political orientation. Some are more effective in Democratic administrations and others during Republican years. But you should never make your decision about retaining a firm solely on this basis of its political strength (or weakness). Washington is a transient town and no effective lobbying organization will be around long if it has not demonstrated an ability to change with the times. Thus, a Republican may be able to effectively represent your issue even if you believe it would be a more Democratic issue.

Remember, party labels are highly deceptive; conservative Democrats often vote with Republicans and liberal Republicans with Democrats.

Since the attorneys you're interviewing will probably not be involved in your day-to-day matters, you should ask them for an opportunity to review the resumes of and meet with those in the firm with whom you would actually be working. They must also be competent and should have a personal rapport with your members.

Finally, you should discuss money. Do not be surprised if the lawyers with whom you speak are reluctant to be precise about the costs of a lobbying campaign. After all, they are not yet totally familiar with either your organization or the difficulties they may encounter as the campaign progresses. You should, however, be able to get a general estimate of total costs. It is best if you do not indicate to the firm whether you think their rough estimate is high, low, or just about right. This is not the time for dickering; that will come later.

At the conclusion of the interview, whether you think it went well or poorly, you should request a written proposal from the firm regarding their ability to perform the necessary work, their strategy, and their estimate of total costs. Unlike public relations firms and professional lobbying firms, it is unlikely that a law firm will send you a proposal for a "contingent fee" based on whether or not the campaign is successful. There are serious ethical questions posed when a lawyer accepts such fees. If a firm does offer a contingent-fee relationship, do not suggest to them that you know such behavior to be unethical—there are rare cases in which is it not—but merely express your surprise that a firm would make such an offer. This should give you an opportunity to see how fast you can get your prospective representatives to blush, or at least explain themselves.

After comparing all the firms on the basis of both your personal interviews and their written proposals, you should present your group with two or three alternatives and conduct a final round of interviews. By this time, the firms should have been thoroughly briefed and you will be in a better position to make an objective choice. Once you have made your decision, however, do not be reluctant to insist that your attorneys continue to represent you aggressively. Remember, they are working for you, not the other way around.

Public Relations Firms

Some public relations firms in Washington offer lobbying services. Although they cannot provide the legal advice often so indispensable to a lobbying campaign, they can sometimes give your group the visibility a traditional Washington law firm cannot. Public relations firms generally can generate press coverage, in the form of either paid advertisements or press conferences—something few law firms are qualified to do. If you believe the best way to reach your target audience is through the media, you should at least consider retaining a public relations firm, either as your sole representative or as an adjunct to other lobbying efforts.

Some public relations firms promote themselves as traditional lobbyists as well as media specialists, but they are the exception. Currently, there are no more than a few dozen individuals at public relations firms who can hope to compete with the better lawyer-lobbyists on the Hill.

As with law firms, you should ask interest groups similar to your own about their public relations contacts and conduct interviews with the candidates according to the guidelines in the previous section. Generally, the presentations given by public relations firms will be much slicker than those of the law firms and may include graphics and dazzling displays of media wizardry. If you are impressed, just be sure to ask what the cost will be for your media campaign.

Independent Lobbying Firms

No one has compiled an accurate listing of all the independent lobbying firms in Washington; as noted earlier, you will not find them listed in the Yellow Pages. They often prefer to be known as "legislative consultants" or "government relations firms," or by some other euphemism. The best way to find these firms is to be referred by organizations that have used them in the past. Usually, major corporations and trade associations are more than willing to give you the names of the independent lobbyists with whom they have worked.

Usually, independent lobbyists are not attorneys, but they have Hill or business experience few lawyers can match. It is not unusual to find independent lobbying firms staffed by former members of Congress and trade association executives with decades of practical legislative experience behind them. Ex-members may even have access to the Senate or House floor, giving them an advantage in last-minute lobbying. Although some lawyers would have you believe the legislative process is so complicated that only a law degree properly qualifies an individual to analyze pending or proposed legislation, the success of independent lobbying firms is proof to the contrary.

In addition, whereas most lawyers bill on an hourly or retainer basis with expenses added, independent lobbying firms often offer a package deal by which all legislative matters of an individual client will be undertaken for a flat fee. Thus, you may be better able to accurately predict costs with an independent lobbying firm.

In short, independent lobbying agencies can offer some services generally unavailable from either law firms or public relations firms. They are a good idea if you want the inside political track and a fixed fee. And unlike lawyers, independent political consultants can ethically accept a contingent fee based upon the outcome of a particular piece of legislation. If they believe the chances of success are good, you may be able to get a results-oriented campaign with real motivation driving your consultant—they don't get paid unless you win. But remember that there is still a chance your campaign will *not* be successful; you should be highly skeptical of any professional lobbyist who claims that a particular result is guaranteed. Lobbying and legislation are just too uncertain a game for this to be possible.

Some lobbying groups cover themselves by retaining independent lobbying firms, law firms, *and* public relations agencies. Although it may be a safe way of covering all the bases, it can be incredibly expensive. If you decide to go this route, you should be sure all the groups you have working for you get along with each other on a personal and professional basis. You don't need to waste your time or money paying for competing firms to work out their differences. It is therefore important that you specify in writing the functions of all groups working for you and provide it to all parties involved. It is also an excellent idea to spend as much time as possible coordinating or at least overseeing the coordination of their activities. Bills can mount rapidly when you have a number of meters running, and some professional lobbyists who feel hurt about not being engaged exclusively would have no compunction about sending their client an inflated bill.

18

THE TEN COMMANDMENTS

"Bad laws are the worst sort of tyranny."

—Edmund Burke

Although the role of a lobbyist may appear extremely complex,* the citizen lobbyist can be effective if he or she follows a few simple rules.

1. Know Your Facts and Be Accurate in Expressing Them

Despite the myth that successful lobbying involves influence peddling, most effective lobbyists trade not in influence but in facts. As a citizen lobbyist, what you may lack in experience and contacts you can make up for in knowledge and research. Accuracy and thoroughness are the hallmarks of successful lobbying campaigns.

During the course of any emotionally charged campaign, there is always a temptation to overstate your case or manufacture statistics to fit your argument. Succumbing to these temptations is almost always ruinous. Even if you win the battle, you may lose the war. Your long term credibility is far more important than any temporary advantage you may gain through prevarication.

2. Know Your Opposition

For every political cause, there will be political opposition. An effective lobbyist will identify the opposition early in a lobbying campaign, fairly and accurately analyze their arguments and power sources, and attempt to neutralize them. At least as much time should be devoted to these activities as to developing your own case.

---

*This book does not even attempt to consider such sophisticated issues as congressional parliamentary procedure, compliance with the Foreign Agents Registration Act, and myriad other topics.

Again, the watchwords of a consistently successful lobbyist are honesty and accuracy. Mischaracterizations of an opponent's position can be as damaging to your own credibility as misstatements of fact in arguing your own case. Rebuttal of opposing positions should go only as far as is necessary to counter your opponents' lobbying efforts.

3. Correct Errors Immediately

Although good lobbyists attempt to be 100 percent accurate in every document or statement they make, errors inevitably creep in. And the more individuals participating in a lobbying campaign, the more likely errors will occur. Thus, it is essential that your organization have firm policies regarding the individuals authorized to speak for the group, the types of commitments these individuals are permitted to make on the group's behalf, the literature and statistics upon which the group bases its arguments, and the procedures to be followed when errors occur.

Mistakes should be corrected as soon as possible after they are discovered. It is not enough merely to admit a mistake was made; your organization must also supply the accurate information at the time it corrects its error. Your degree of public acknowledgment of the error should be dictated by the seriousness of the mistake. Usually, warning those who received the inaccurate information that it should not be relied on and correcting the mistake in as low-key a manner as possible will be enough. It is always embarrassing to admit you're wrong, but it is political suicide if you don't. You can put a good face on errors, but do not attempt to cover them up, particularly if your allies are relying on the information you have supplied.

4. Plan, Coordinate, and Follow Up on Each Contact

An enormous amount of time, energy, and intellect is wasted each year by lobbyists who have not carefully planned their approach to the Hill. Each contact you make with a congressional office should be thoroughly researched in advance, careful notes should be kept of the content and results of meetings, and each meeting should be followed up with additional written memoranda.

It does a lobbyist little good to develop a network of congressional allies and then not use them. Friends should be kept fully informed of your activities, their questions and comments should be promptly addressed, and above all, they should be thanked for their contribution to your cause. Your skill and diligence in using your contacts will be a measure of your success.

5. Avoid Zealotry

The more strongly you feel about an issue, the more important it is to be aware of the danger of zealotry. Fanaticism neither impresses nor convinces many people in Washington. Symptoms of zealotry include misrepresenting your opponents' views, underestimating your opposition, believing and saying that your opponents are motivated by unethical and even immoral instincts, and finally, overstating your own case. Zealotry is the enemy of credibility, the lobbyist's greatest asset. It is one thing to be an aggressive advocate, quite another to replace rational argument with slogans.

An important corollary to this rule is to never show anger when you fail to persuade a member of Congress of the righteousness of your cause. You must live for another day, another fight. Anger does your connections no good, and can make you less valuable in the future.

6. Cultivate Your Allies; Make Sure They Do Their Part

There is hardly an issue in Washington that does not attract a number of groups for widely different reasons. Your chances of succeeding in a lobbying campaign will be enormously enhanced if you join with other groups who share your aims. Allies don't just happen; they must be sought out and cultivated. In the nation's capital you are likely to find them in the most unlikely places—even among groups that have traditionally opposed you. Keep your eye on the ultimate objective of the lobbying campaign, not the positions or personalities of your allies.

Merely gaining allies, however, is not enough. You must be sure they do their part. Specifically, make sure your friends keep their promises and abide by the same standards of credibility and integrity you set for yourself. Announce in writing specific goals and projects each group will be expected to perform. Make sure you keep your part of the deal and they keep theirs.

7. Know the Legislative Process

All the good intentions, careful planning, research, and alliances will do you little good unless you understand the legislative process—the rules by which the game is played. Few people, even members of Congress, are regarded as parliamentary experts on all aspects of congressional procedure, but as a lobbyist you have an obligation to be at least as familiar with the rules as the people employing them on the floor of the Senate and the House. In addition, since the clear intent of the Congress is often subverted by overzealous (or underzealous) bureaucrats, it is equally important that you understand what happens to laws *after* they are passed.

8. Be Frugal with Your Money

You have no doubt read of professional lobbying campaigns that cost hundreds of thousands of dollars. These efforts are mounted by sophisticated pressure groups with more money than good sense. Be very judicious about how you spend your funds, particularly when you retain outside consultants or attorneys. Sometimes they are absolutely necessary, but be sure you get your money's worth.

9. Grow Thick Skin

You don't have to be a cynic to be a successful Washington lobbyist, but a healthy degree of skepticism helps. You also should develop an immunity to petty insults; you must not allow temporary setbacks to ruin your concentration, and you must not take any of the attacks on your position personally. You must understand that the fire aimed in your direction is merely business. Although you should take your job seriously, you can't afford to take yourself too seriously in a lobbying campaign. Above all, maintain your sense of humor. You'll need it.

10. Win

No one should become involved in lobbying as an academic exercise. Lobbying is serious business that can affect thousands of people's lives and the way our country is run. People in Washington don't necessarily object to amateurs, but you will find few who will tolerate those who squander the rights of petition and redress. You are expected to take your role seriously—to be dedicated to winning and not merely to "playing the game."

No matter how remote your chances of success may appear, you must not deviate from your commitment. This is one factor that separates the citizen lobbyist from the professional. Some career lobbyists are merely hired guns who go from one issue to the next with little personal stake in the outcome. The citizen lobbyist is almost always a deeply committed individual who really believes in what he or she is doing. Strength of conviction is what offsets the enormous financial advantage enjoyed by some of the huge special interest lobbies. Not only that, but winning is always more fun than losing.

19

RESOURCES

The purpose of this book is to give you a general idea of lobbying techniques. It is only an instruction manual; to do an adequate job at lobbying you will need the proper tools. This chapter will help you choose the right tools for the job.

Seminars

Brookings Institute

The Brookings Institute offers a series of seminars entitled "Inside Congress: Understanding the Legislative Process." These four-day seminars are intensive examinations of how the Congress shapes major national policies, how you can impact congressional policy makers, and what issues are currently engaging the Congress. These seminars also provide access to an invaluable network of other lobbyists, government officials, and congressional liaisons.

Peter Schoettle
(202) 797-6094
pschoettle@brookings.edu
www.brookings.edu/execed/open/in_congress101.htm
Cost: $1,850

American League of Lobbyists

The American League of Lobbyists (ALL) conducts numerous seminars and other training programs on lobbying, media relations, congressional communications, the Lobbying Disclosure Act, and related subjects. The organization awards Professional Lobbying Certificates (PLCs) to individuals who complete a 14-session course in various aspects of the legislative process.

American League of Lobbyists
(703) 960-3011
alldc.org@erols.com
Cost: $105 per session for members; $205 per session for nonmembers

Reference Manuals

Congressional Directory

Almost every lobbyist's office in Washington has one of these official directories, but better manuals are available from private sources. About the only thing unique about the directory is the section containing congressional district maps. Congressional staffs change so rapidly that by the time the *Congressional Directory* is published, it is out of date. For the price, however, it is a good starting point; it is a traditional part of every lobbyist's library. The Government Printing Office (GPO) sells hard copies and offers free access to an online edition, though the latter is updated irregularly.

Government Printing Office
732 North Capitol Street NW
Washington, DC 20401
(866) 512-1800 (toll-free)
(202) 512-1800 (D.C. area)
www.gpoaccess.gov/cdirectory/index.html
Cost: $39

Congressional Staff Directory

The *Congressional Staff Directory* is privately published by Congressional Quarterly and provides a more thorough cross-indexing of congressional offices, committee assignments, etc. than the *Congressional Directory*. Although it lacks the congressional district maps, it is generally a more useful guide to the members of Congress themselves.

Congressional Staff Directory
1255 22nd Street NW, Suite 400
Washington, DC 20037
(866) 427-7737 (toll-free)
(202) 729-1800 (D.C. area)
directorysales@cqpress.com
www.cqpress.com
Cost: $429

Almanac of American Politics

The *Almanac of American Politics* provides a reasonably comprehensive analysis of each member of Congress, including a thumbnail sketch of the member's state or district, his or her voting record, and ratings by various interest groups (e.g., Americans for Democratic Action). These groups' ratings will give you an idea of the member's basic proclivity—moderate, liberal, conservative. Do not, however, be dissuaded from approaching a member merely because his or her general voting pattern may not seem friendly to your cause. The almanac should merely serve as a guide to the political leanings of congressmen and senators. The *Almanac of American Politics* is unique in the type of analysis it provides and is an extremely valuable resource tool.

National Journal Group
P.O. Box 96157
Washington, DC 20090-6157
(800) 356-4838
service@nationaljournal.com
https://secure.nationaljournal.com/ALM2006
Cost: $55.96

Congressional Yellow Book

The *Congressional Yellow Book* is a congressional directory published by Leadership Directories, Inc. Once you purchase a subscription, you receive updates several times a year to reflect recent changes in congressional staff and committee assignments. Since these changes occur with what some would regard as alarming regularity, the *Congressional Yellow Book* is probably the most useful day-to-day resource book you can have in your library. Although it is relatively expensive, it can save you hours when you need to track down the right staff member for your problem. The *Yellow Book* also includes information on all special interest caucuses (e.g., Black Caucus, Steel Caucus), unavailable in this format in any other publication. In short, the *Congressional Yellow Book* is the single most valuable tool you can have; it is highly recommended.

Leadership Directories
1001 G Street NW, Suite 200 East
Washington, DC 20001
(202) 347-7757 (phone)
(202) 628-3430 (fax)
www.leadershipdirectories.com/products/cyb.htm
Cost: $450 for a year's subscription

Federal Yellow Book

The *Federal Yellow Book* is also published by Leadership Directories, Inc. It provides up-to-date listings of virtually the entire bureaucracy of the executive branch. Its loose-leaf format enables you to update it on a regular basis, and it is very useful in helping you penetrate the bureaucratic maze. Although it is somewhat intimidating in appearance, it is much easier to use than official government telephone books and is accurate about 80 percent of the time—a remarkable achievement given the constant changes within the system. If any significant portion of your lobbying activities involves contacts within the executive branch, the *Federal Yellow Book* is a must.

Leadership Directories
1001 G Street NW, Suite 200 East
Washington, DC 20001
(202) 347-7757 (phone)
(202) 628-3430 (fax)
www.leadershipdirectories.com/products/fyb.htm
Cost: $450 for a year's subscription

Washington Representatives

This softbound directory lists most of the major special interest groups in Washington, together with their addresses, telephone numbers, and the principal lobbyists who represent them. The directory is cross-indexed by representatives and clients so you can determine, for example, which law firms represent whom. (Some groups, of course, have their own lobbyists, who are listed as well.) Although it is about the most thorough directory of its kind, it is not comprehensive. In fact, it barely scratches the surface of the labyrinthine world of Washington representation. Further, the directory is replete with errors, so it cannot be relied on as definitive. Still, it's the only such directory available, and you should have one in your library.

Columbia Books
8120 Woodmont Avenue, Suite 110
Bethesda, MD 20814
(202) 464-1662
www.columbiabooks.com (online orders)
http://lobbyists.info (subscription-based online access)
Cost: $699 for a year's subscription; $3,000 for a premium subscription

Hudson's Washington News Media Contacts Directory

Hudson's lists all media correspondents by the publication they represent, cross-indexed by correspondent name, location, and other factors. It is an indispensable tool if you are planning any sort of media campaign—it should provide you with a good starting point for developing a list for press releases.

Hudson's Washington News Media Contacts Directory
738 Main Street, Suite 447
Waltham, MA 02451
(781) 647-3200
www.hudsonsdirectory.com
Cost: $329 for a year's subscription, including online access

Pocket Manuals

Pocket manuals that detail congressional organization are available from a number of trade associations and labor unions. Any attempt to enumerate all of them would invariably miss some, so a prospective lobbyist should inquire with related interest groups to see whether they have produced their own specialized pocket manuals. Some of the better-known manuals are published by the U.S. Chamber of Commerce, the AFL-CIO, and the American Mining Congress. These books are sometimes available only to association or union members, but a direct inquiry by nonmembers is often rewarded. These pocket manuals are much handier than the reference books cited previously and can be carried in your pocket or briefcase.

U.S. Chamber of Commerce
1615 H Street NW
Washington, DC 20062
www.uschamber.com

AFL-CIO
815 16th Street NW
Washington, DC 20006
www.aflcio.org

National Mining Association
101 Constitution Avenue NW, Suite 500 East
Washington, DC 20001-2133
www.nma.org

Standing Rules of the Senate; Rules of the House of Representatives

These two publications are the equivalents of *Robert's Rules of Order* for the House and the Senate. Each body has its own rules, which differ in significant respects. Do not attempt to read these books cover to cover; a literal reading is almost inherently misleading. However, an understanding of the rules is useful when your tactics involve sophisticated parliamentary maneuvering, so these publications belong on your resource shelf to be consulted when necessary. One caveat: the rules of the House and Senate are subject to change, so you should be sure to get the current year's versions. They are available from the clerk of the House of Representatives and the secretary of the Senate, respectively.

Clerk
United States House of Representatives
Washington, DC 20515
http://rules.house.gov/ruleprec/house_rules.htm

Secretary
United States Senate
Washington, DC 20510
http://rules.senate.gov/senaterules

Congressional ZIP Code Directory

In preparing any grassroots letter-writing campaign, it is essential that you know which members of Congress represent your constituents. In states in which there is only one congressman (e.g., North Dakota), the job is relatively easy. In more populous areas, however, it is extremely difficult to determine exactly which congressional districts contain the greatest concentration of your supporters. Capitol Advantage provides a solution for this problem—a free online database of ZIP codes cross-referenced by the congressional district each one belongs to. All you have to do to determine where your greatest power lies is to enter your supporters' ZIP codes into the search engine. The service provides a list of the senators and representative for each ZIP code, as well as information on how each member has voted on recent legislation. This directory is absolutely essential if you plan to do any grassroots lobbying.

Capitol Advantage
www.congress.org

Catalog of U.S. Government Publications

The Government Printing Office maintains an online database of documents published by the federal government. In presenting any lobbying campaign on the Hill, government studies and data are usually given great credibility. In this database you should be able to find a government publication supporting virtually any position you wish to take. Simply go to the Government Printing Office's Web site and locate the input box labeled "Catalog of U.S. Government Publications." Enter a search query for the issue you are interested in and the search engine will bring up any document related to that issue. Many of the publications are available for free online, or they can be procured at a reasonable price either in person or by mail.

Government Printing Office
732 North Capitol Street NW
Washington, DC 20401
(866) 512-1800 (toll-free)
(202) 512-1800 (D.C. area)
www.gpoaccess.gov

Periodicals

Congressional Quarterly

CQ is one of the periodicals relied on most by Washington insiders. Although it is relatively expensive, its articles—on the status of legislation, personalities and committee jurisdiction, and other important topics—are essential to an effective lobbying campaign, and are not duplicated by any other publication. Despite its title, CQ is published on a weekly basis and is well worth the cost. Its Web site offers a variety of subscription options.

Congressional Quarterly
1255 22nd Street NW, Suite 400
Washington, DC 20037
www.cq.com

National Journal

The National Journal is a specialized political publication with its greatest readership in the Washington area, particularly among lobbyists. Like CQ, National Journal concentrates on in-depth stories regarding pending and proposed legislation, status of committee and subcommittee action, hard news about political personalities, and other stories useful to lobbyists. In addition, *National Journal* provides summaries of committee action and legislative calendars, both of which are sometimes more up-to-date than even the back pages of the *Congressional Record*, which purport to carry the same information. *National Journal* also includes analyses of administrative action, and it is well worth its relatively high price.

National Journal Group
600 New Hampshire Avenue NW
Washington, DC 20037
www.nationaljournal.com

Bureau of National Affairs

The Bureau of National Affairs (BNA) is a nonpartisan research organization that publishes a number of specialized newsletters (e.g., *Environment Reporter, International Trade Daily*) in almost all fields affected directly by legislation. The BNA reports, although rather costly, include specialized information on topics of interest to your group that you will be unable to find in most other publications. A full list of current BNA publications, together with descriptions and sample issues, is available online or by contacting the BNA.

Bureau of National Affairs
1231 25th Street NW
Washington, DC 20037
(800) 372-1033
www.bna.com

Kiplinger Letter

The *Kiplinger Letter* is one of the most highly advertised newsletters in Washington. Its spare style and immediacy set it apart from other, similar publications. Kiplinger also publishes a number of specialized newsletters that follow the same style. Although not specifically designed for lobbyists, the Kiplinger letter provides fast, usually accurate thumbnail advisories on issues that may be important to you.

Kiplinger
1729 H Street NW
Washington, DC 20006
www.kiplinger.com

Trade Association and Interest Group Publications

In Washington, virtually every trade association and special interest group with a membership of more than three has a trade publication. Sometimes these publications are limited to members, but often membership costs are low enough that you may want to join a relevant organization just to receive the publication. Publications range from the sophisticated to the juvenile; you would be well advised to review a copy or two before you make the decision to subscribe. For further information, contact the interest groups listed in *Washington Representatives* (see "Reference Manuals," above), or visit the American Society of Association Executives (ASAE) library.

American Society of Association Executives
1575 I Street NW
Washington, DC 20005

Other Special Interest Publications

At last count, there were over fifteen thousand newspapers, magazines, and newsletters being published in the United States on subjects ranging from skydiving to embryology. No matter how arcane your issue, most likely there is at least one publication that specializes in it. Even if you disagree with the editorial policies of the publication in your field, it is always a good idea to subscribe. After all, you should know even the myths that are being circulated about your issue. Often, free copies of these publications are distributed on the Hill.

Newspaper of Note

In addition to keeping up with specialized publications, most Washington lobbyists begin their morning by reading the *Washington Post*, the *New York Times*, and the *Wall Street Journal*. Even if you believe that your issue is not likely to be covered in depth by these publications, they contain politically sensitive stories that few effective lobbyists can afford to ignore.

Washington Post
1150 15th Street NW
Washington, DC 20071
www.washingtonpost.com

New York Times
229 West 43rd Street
New York, NY 10036
www.nytimes.com

Wall Street Journal
200 Liberty Street
New York, NY 10281
www.wsj.com

Governmental Material

During the course of any lobbying campaign, you will need a small library on the current law, applicable regulations, and the status of pending legislation. Although there are numerous private companies that will provide you with in-depth, sophisticated resource documents, you can usually get this information from the government itself, at prices significantly below those offered by private companies.

THOMAS

The Library of Congress maintains a very good Web site with an abundance of information on bill status and current legislation, with cross-links to other resources. Using various search engines, you can track multiple bills; check the status of a bill, including mark-ups, revisions, and major actions; and find committee reports and congressional records. The format is very user-friendly, making it easy to stay updated.

THOMAS
http://thomas.loc.gov

Congressional Record

The *Record*, as described in chapter 9, contains the minutes of congressional debates. It is published daily during the congressional sessions and is relatively inexpensive given its bulk (three to four hundred pages a day). Almost every lobbyist, however, accesses the *Record* online at THOMAS (see above).

Federal Register

The *Federal Register* is published daily, except weekends and holidays, and includes notices from all federal regulatory and administrative agencies about administrative hearings, decisions, proposed rules, and all other bureaucratic action. Many of the notices are required by law and may be legally binding. Even if you feel you are only interested in legislation (as opposed to regulation), you cannot afford to be without the *Register*. Subscriptions are available through the Government Printing Office; online access is free at the GPO Web site.

Government Printing Office
732 North Capitol Street NW
Washington, DC 20401
(866) 512-1800 (toll-free)
(202) 512-1800 (D.C. area)
www.gpoaccess.gov/fr/index.html

Hearings and Reports

During the legislative process, the various congressional committees that consider a particular bill will publish transcripts of their hearings and other information submitted for the record. If you order them through the Government Printing Office, there will be a charge (usually less than two dollars), but you can almost always get them free from the committees themselves. Unlike the *Congressional Record* and the *Federal Register*, transcripts are published irregularly, usually months after the hearings actually take place. Transcripts of prior hearings are also available from either the committee that conducted the hearings or the GPO, but if you need hearings going back a number of years, you will have to contact the Library of Congress and pay a substantial reproduction fee.

Committee reports are also published irregularly, but usually soon after the committee in question has made its decisions regarding a piece of legislation. These reports are a much better guide to legislative history than are the transcripts of hearings, as they represent the opinion of the Congress itself regarding the legislation in question. Committee reports on legislation affecting your subject matter are an essential part of your library. They can be acquired (usually at no cost) from the committee or the GPO.

Government Printing Office
732 North Capitol Street NW
Washington, DC 20401
(866) 512-1800 (toll-free)
(202) 512-1800 (D.C. area)
www.gpoaccess.gov

Bills and Committee Prints

When a bill is introduced, copies are made available almost immediately to the public at no charge. They can be obtained from the clerk of the House of Representatives and the secretary of the Senate, both of whom are located in the Capitol Building. After a bill has been partially "marked up" to include amendments, technical corrections, etc., a revised version of the bill will be published under the designation "Committee Print." The committee print will indicate any changes from the original version of the bill by putting a single line through any deleted text and italicizing added text.

In tracking the progress of any legislation, it is essential you obtain the most recent version. There are delivery services in Washington that will pick them up if you do not have your own messengers (see "Services" below). The clerk of the House and secretary of the Senate will also mail you these versions upon request. Most often, however, lobbyists rely on the online versions of bills available from THOMAS (http://thomas.loc.gov).

Clerk
United States House of Representatives
Washington, DC 20515

Secretary
United States Senate
Washington, DC 20510

United States Code

The *United States Code* (and a privately published version, *United States Code Annotated*) includes the body of federal law. The entire set comprises dozens of volumes, each costing up to $90 each, but unless you are planning to practice law or are very rich, you need only purchase the volume(s) directly affecting your issue that you think you will rely on the most. If there are other provision in the *Code* that you think might be useful, you can access them for free online.

Because federal law changes so quickly, it is essential that you update your copies on a regular basis. The *United States Code Annotated* (*USCA*), available from West Publishing, includes a yearly "pocket" element that slides into the rear cover. *USCA* also provides a cursory legislative history of each title and section of the code, and a list of court cases explaining each provision of the law. *USCA* is a useful tool in determining what the law actually means (despite what it may say), but you should be careful not to rely exclusively upon its opinions. If you have questions regarding the interpretation of legislation, consult an attorney.

Individual titles of the *United States Code* are available from the Government Printing Office, and the full text may be accessed on several different Web sites. Be warned: you will want to have some idea what you are looking for, as the *United States Code* is quite lengthy.

West Publishing
(800) 344-5008
http://west.thomson.com

Government Printing Office
732 North Capitol Street NW
Washington, DC 20401
(866) 512-1800 (toll-free)
(202) 512-1800 (D.C. area)
http://bookstore.gpo.gov/subjects/sb-197.jsp (online orders)
www.gpoaccess.gov/uscode/index.html (free online access)

Cornell Law School
www4.law.cornell.edu/uscode (free online access)

Code of Federal Regulations

The *Code of Federal Regulations* (CFR) incorporates all the technical interpretations of statutes as construed by the bureaucrats of the executive branch, and it is critical to virtually every lobbying effort. As with the *United States Code*, it makes economical sense to purchase just the CFR volumes you will use the most and look up any other references online. Never rely on an outdated CFR in presenting your case, as regulations change even more frequently than statutes. Most volumes are republished on an annual basis and reflect the changes made during the preceding year. Individual volumes of CFR may be obtained from the Government Printing Office, and the full text may be accessed for free on the office's Web site.

Government Printing Office
732 North Capitol Street NW
Washington, DC 20401
(866) 512-1800 (toll-free)
(202) 512-1800 (D.C. area)
www.gpoaccess.gov/cfr/index.html

Other Legal Publications

There are literally dozens of publicly and privately published legal treatises, encyclopedias, services, etc. that interpret existing statutes. Most of them are expensive and are designed for use by lawyers. If you have specific questions about the interpretation of the law, it is usually cheaper, easier, faster, and safer to request an attorney to prepare a memorandum of law for you on a specific subject than to attempt to subscribe to all of these publications.

Undoubtedly, this advice will be challenged not only by the publishers of law books, but also by lobbyists who have their own favorite legal resources. As you gain more expertise in the field, undoubtedly you will form your own opinions.

Study Committees and Special Interest Caucuses

In both houses of the Congress, study or policy committees and special interest caucuses publish analyses of pending and proposed legislation. These analyses are usually slanted toward the view of the particular committee or caucus concerned—but that is sometimes what you want. Whereas the neutral tone of many privately published journals is fine when you are preparing your facts, you also have to know the arguments on both sides of the question. To find out what your supporters and opponents are saying on the Hill, contact the relevant special interest caucus or study group.

There are more than fifty caucuses in the House, ranging from the Arts Caucus to the Wind Hazard Reduction Caucus. The Senate only has about a dozen, but they tend to be a bit broader in scope. Although a few of the best-known groups are listed below, check the *Congressional Yellow Book* to see if a special interest caucus has been formed in your field.

Bear in mind, some of the groups below may only exist when a particular party has the majority, and contact information may change with alarming regularity—sometimes week to week. The information given below is correct as of this writing, but you may have to track down the appropriate group yourself. Find the member who chairs the particular group you are looking for and contact his or her office. Remember the tips for talking to congressional staffers listed in chapter 11. Respect and a pleasant disposition go a long way.

Senate Democratic Conference
(202) 224-3735
http://democrats.senate.gov

Senate Republican Policy Committee
347 Russell Senate Office Building
Washington, DC 20510
(202) 224-2946
www.senate.gov/~rpc

Senate Democratic Policy Committee
419 Hart Senate Office Building
Washington, DC 20510
(202) 224-3232
http://democrats.senate.gov/dpc

House Republican Conference
1420 Longworth House Office Building
Washington, DC 20515
(202) 225-5107
www.gop.gov

House Republican Policy Committee
411 Cannon Building
Washington, DC 20515
(202) 225-6168
http://policy.house.gov

House Democratic Caucus
202A Cannon House Office Building
Washington, DC 20515
http://democrats.house.gov

House Republican Study Committee (Conservative)
(202) 226-8582
rsc@mail.house.gov
www.house.gov/hensarling/rsc

Whip Notices

A "whip" is a senator or congressman elected by his party colleagues to, among other things, ensure that party members attend important votes. (The name implies that, as a party officer, this person "whips" his or her members into line.) The majority and minority whips of both houses publish "whip notices" on a daily basis during the legislative session. Professional lobbyists rely on them on extensively, because they provide an indication of what the congressional leadership thinks will happen during a particular legislative day. Although they are available by mail, their real value lies in their immediacy. You would be well advised to have them picked up by a messenger if you are in the thick of a legislative duel. You can also search for whip notices at various members' Web sites, especially in the Senate.

The contact information below is accurate as of this writing, but may change depending on party leadership and the congressional balance of power.

Senate Majority Whip
309 Hart Senate Office Building
Washington, DC 20510
(202) 224-2152
http://durbin.senate.gov/index.cfm

Senate Minority Whip
487 Russell Senate Office Building
Washington, DC 20510
(202) 224-6253
http://lott.senate.gov

House Majority Whip
H-329 Capitol Building
Washington, DC 20515
(202) 226-3210
http://majoritywhip.house.gov

House Minority Whip
H-307 Capitol Building
Washington, DC 20515
(202) 225-0197
http://minoritywhip.house.gov

KnowLegis

KnowLegis, a company managed by Capitol Advantage, has an online service that sends alerts to subscribers regarding congressional press releases, staff changes, town hall meetings, and any appearance in the news by a member of Congress.

KnowLegis
2751 Prosperity Avenue, Suite 600
Fairfax, VA 22031
(703) 289-9816
www.knowlegis.net

Status of Legislation

Bill Status Offices

Both the House and the Senate maintain offices that analyze the status of all pending bills. The service is free, and you can determine the status of any legislation by calling the Capitol and requesting the respective Bill Status Office.

Capitol Switchboard
(202) 224-3121

Floor Information

During the legislative session, the party Cloak Rooms in both houses of the Congress maintain recorded updates on the actions taking place on the House and Senate floors. These recorded messages are updated several times daily, and you can call twenty-four hours a day. This service is particularly useful in planning last-minute strategy. It is also a good way to get current information on the passage or defeat of legislation.

House Republican Cloak Room
(202) 225-7430

House Democratic Cloak Room
(202) 225-7400

Senate Republican Cloak Room
(202) 224-8601

Senate Democratic Cloak Room
(202) 224-8541

Other Sources

THOMAS (http://thomas.loc.gov) also tracks an exhaustive collection of bills and updates their status frequently. Click on "Bills, Resolutions," and from there you can locate the bill you desire using a plethora of search criteria.

Many administrative agencies also maintain dial-a-regulation tapes in which recent agency action is communicated. Since the telephone numbers for these services change frequently, you should call the main switchboard number of the agency in question for the current listing.

Political Blogs

Web logs ("blogs") have become something of a phenomenon in the past few years. No one knows exactly how many political blogs exist, but they surely number in the thousands. Engaging with the blogosphere is a good way to increase the visibility of your cause. Most blogs have feedback forms or forums through which you can join the point/counterpoint discussions in your spare time (or your members can do so in theirs). Another technique is to provide the webmasters or "blog czars" (many of them have zany titles) with your materials. Sometimes you can even convince bloggers to provide direct links to your own Web site (often in exchange for reciprocal links).

Blogs can be very useful, but like booze, a little can go a long way. It is very easy to become so engrossed in the blogosphere that you lose all perspective on your real task—getting legislation passed or defeated. To use blogs effectively, choose your targets carefully. Blogs unashamedly borrow material from one another, so if you want to have the biggest impact, focus on the ones that are the most highly regarded. Some of the very best as of this writing are listed below.

If you are looking for specialized blogs that cater to a particular audience, visit www.campaignline.com/blogs, *Campaign & Elections* magazine's political blog directory. This site features a searchable index of hundreds of blogs on any conceivable subject.

The quality and relevance of blogs change with astonishing rapidity, so the best blog on Tuesday may be passé by Wednesday morning. Always keep in mind that just because something appears on the Internet does not automatically render it credible.

www.nationalreview.com
www.lileks.com
www.wonkette.com
www.instapundit.com
www.littlegreenfootballs.com
www.andrewsullivan.com
www.talkingpointsmemo.com
www.oxblog.com

Services

Clipping Services

Clipping services are not cheap, but they can sometimes be a valuable asset in addition to your regular subscriptions. As discussed in chapter 5, they will review any publications you select and clip articles pertaining to subjects in which you are interested. Clipping services are listed in the Yellow Pages, but you should seek recommendations from people who have used them before you sign any contracts. Listed below is one such service, which has delivered adequately in the past for some major lobbying firms.

Burrelles*Luce*
75 East Northfield Road
Livingston, New Jersey 07039
(800) 631-1160
www.burrellesluce.com

Press Services

For a fee, PR Newswire will put your press releases into a nationwide distribution network accessed by newspapers all over the country. Many papers, particularly those outside of major metropolitan areas, will carry these releases as filler stories. You can also ask PR Newswire to distribute your releases to specific regions of the country at considerably reduced cost.

PR Newswire
810 7th Avenue, 32nd Floor
New York, NY 10019
(888) 776-0942

Delivery Services

Washington is unique in a number of respects, but perhaps the strangest is its reliance on delivery services. It's not that the mail service is so bad, just that having materials hand-delivered has become a Washington tradition. Everything, it seems, must be delivered yesterday.

Eventually every law firm with more than five people hires its own messenger, and at least a dozen private delivery firms offer two-hour delivery of any package in town. Messengers are also useful in picking up packages from the Hill, the Government Printing Office, the clerk of the House, and the secretary of the Senate. Senate and House committees are notorious for not sending promised bills, reports, etc., so messenger pickups become indispensable.

The reliance on messengers is so deeply ingrained in Washington that workers in Hill offices sometimes feel you don't deserve it if you don't pick it up. Some of the better-known messenger services are listed on the next page.

Washington Express
12240 Indian Creed Court #100
Beltsville, MD 20705
(301) 210-3500

Quick Messenger Service
4829 Fairmont Avenue, Suite B
Bethesda, MD 20814
(240) 223-2233

LaserShip
1522 K Street NW
Washington, DC 20005
(202) 347-7663

Hotels

Washington hotels are overbooked much of the time. Therefore, it is always advisable to reserve a room well in advance. Although the ratings of hotels go up and down, prices only go up. Rather than attempt to list all the hotels in Washington, I suggest you contact the Visitors Information Association, which can provide a comprehensive up-to-date list of all the hotels in the area.

Visitors Information Association
1212 New York Avenue NW
Washington, DC 20005-3987
(202) 789-7000

Restaurants

For years, Washington was regarded by epicureans as a gastronomical wasteland. Whether that was ever true is a subject of some debate, but it is certainly not an accurate analysis today. In fact, lunch—with a member of Congress, a member of the congressional staff, or another lobbyist—is a Washington lobbying tradition.

Remember, buying lunch for a member of Congress or staffer is essentially forbidden by the most recent ethics rules. This has caused a slight downturn in the lunch crowds at some Hill restaurants, but senators and congressmen still seem to fill plenty of chairs at the better eateries. They usually pick up their own portions of the checks, either by charging them to their campaign committees or by paying for them out of their own pockets—about half of the members of Congress are millionaires. Remember, however, that staffers are rarely in the millionaires' club, and be wary of inviting these folks to an expensive lunch unless special circumstances such as a fundraiser allow you to pick up the check (and be careful even in those cases to get firm clearance before you pay). Other lobbyists, of course, are under no such ethical restraints, and many have expense accounts which allow for some really good meals.

A number of excellent restaurant guides are available, perhaps the best being the annual issue of *Washingtonian* magazine (www.washingtonian.com) that rates area restaurants.

Metro

In Washington, public transportation consists of an interconnected system of subways and buses called Metro. It is by far the fastest and cheapest way to get around town, particularly in winter and during rush hour. If you are familiar with other subway systems, don't be dismayed. The Washington system is clean, fast, and safe.

Washington Metropolitan Transit Authority
600 5th Street NW
Washington, DC 20001
(202) 962-1234
www.wmata.com

Taxis

The Washington cab system is a throwback to another era. Washington taxis do not have meters; you are charged based on the "zones" you travel through. Each cab carries a zone map behind the driver, but you have to have been born in Washington to decipher it. Fares are relatively inexpensive, but there is ample opportunity for fudging. If you are unfamiliar with the geography, ask the driver how much the fare will be before you set out. (During rush hour, you must also pay a surcharge.) If there is any dispute about your fare, do not be reluctant to call the cops. They are very experienced in taxi shakedowns.

District drivers may pick up other fares on the way to your destination as long as it does not take you more than four blocks out of your way. Your fare will not be affected by picking up other riders, but you may be delayed. Drivers are also reluctant to go to certain destinations in Washington, particularly in the northeast quadrant and in Anacostia. If you must go to one of these areas, get in the cab and close the door—then tell the driver where you are going. If the driver refuses, suggest that you will write to the taxicab commission. Drivers tend to be more accommodating to forceful people.

Despite the complexity of the Washington cab system, taxis are readily available, and because parking on the Hill is impossible, they and Metro have a monopoly on transportation there.

Office Space

Washington is one of the tightest real estate markets in the country; less than 0.5 percent of office space is available at any given time. Space is outrageously expensive in the downtown area—twenty to fifty dollars per square foot per year. If you intend on setting up an office in Washington, you might initially decide to rent space on Capitol Hill, where rents are somewhat more reasonable and the location is very convenient to both houses of the Congress. If you plan on a permanent office in Washington, you should consult commercial real estate brokers.

You can also hire "office planning consultants" who can help you set up an entire office, including telephones, furniture, stationery, and the thousands of other details that can frustrate even the most unflappable people. Check the phone book, or ask other interest groups for recommendations; these consultants are often located through word of mouth. Before retaining particular consultants, be sure to ask them whether they are "full service"—i.e., whether they will not only arrange for furniture, but take care of all the other details as well. You should not expect an interior designer or office furniture company to perform the services outlined here.

Other Services and Materials

There are several adequate publications that list providers of office materials and services. The manuals are basically advertising directories, so read their claims with a note of caution. These directories can be secured from the regional board of trade.

Greater Washington Board of Trade
1725 I Street NW, Suite 200
Washington, DC 20006
(202) 857-5900
www.bot.org

Books on Lobbying

Barnes, Robert A., et al. *The Washington Lobby*. Washington, D.C.: Congressional Quarterly, 1971.

Choate, Pat. *Agents of Influence*. New York: Knopf, 1990.

Eastman, Hope. *Lobbying: A Constitutionally Protected Right*. Washington, D.C.: American Enterprise Institute for Public Policy Research, 1977.

Gecan, Michael. *Going Public: An Organizer's Guide to Citizen Action*. New York: Anchor Books, 2004.

Gerston, Larry N. *Public Policy Making: Process and Principles*. Armonk, N.Y.: M.E. Sharpe, 1997.

Hague, Barry N., and Brian D. Loader, eds. *Digital Democracy: Discourse and Decision Making in the Information Age*. London: Routledge, 1999.

Howe, Russell Warren, and Sara Hays Trott. *The Power Peddlers*. Garden City, N.Y.: Doubleday, 1977.

Lane, Edgar. *Lobbying and the Law*. Berkeley: University of California Press, 1964.

Martin Ryan Haley & Associates. *Campaign Contributions and Lobbying Laws (Condensed)*. Arlington, Va.: Federal State Reports, 1978.

Murphy, Thomas P. *Pressures upon Congress: Legislation by Lobby*. Woodbury, N.Y.: Barron's Educational Series, 1973.

National Association of Bar Executives. *Manual of Legislative Techniques*. Chicago: NABE, 1975.

Nownes, Anthony J. *Pressure and Power: Organized Interests in American Politics*. Boston: Houghton Mifflin, 2001.

Peters, Charles. *How Washington Really Works*. 4th ed. N.p.: Basic Books, 1993.

Schlozman, Kay, and John Tierney. *Organized Interests and American Democracy*. New York: Harper & Row, 1986.

Segell, J. Peter, ed. *A Summary of Lobbying Disclosure Laws and Regulations in the Fifty States*. Washington, D.C.: Plus Publications, 1979.

Smucker, Bob. *The Nonprofit Lobbying Guide*. 2nd ed. Washington, D.C.: Independent Sector, 1999.

Special Committee on Election Laws. *Campaign and Lobbying Law Handbook*. Los Angeles: Los Angeles County Bar Association, 1976.

House Committee on the Judiciary. *Lobbying Accountability and Transparency Act of 2006*. 109th Congress, 2nd sess., 2006. H. Rep. 109-439.

Webster, George D., and Frederick J. Krebs. *Associations & Lobbying Regulation: A Guide for Non-profit Organizations*. Washington, D.C.: Association Division, Chamber of Commerce of the United States, 1979.

Wright, John R. *Interest Groups and Congress: Lobbying, Contributions, and Influence*. New York: Longman, 2003.

INDEX

A

AAs. *See* administrative assistants
action plan
  clearance procedures in, 22–23
  congressional contacts section of, 23–24
  demonstrations section of, 25–26
  developing, 21
  gimmicks section of, 27
  Hill blitz section of, 27–28
  importance of, 28
  letters section of, 24
  press contacts in, 22
  press relations section of, 21–23
acts. *See* laws
administrative agencies
  allies in, 99–101
  approaching, 100
  decision-making in, 101
  documenting in resource book, 19
  exploiting competition among, 18
  identifying and approaching, 17–18
  influencing, 100–101
  obtaining directory of, 168
administrative assistants (AAs)
  interacting with, 80–81
  roles and responsibilities of, 79–80
advertising, 29–30
agencies. *See* administrative agencies
ALL (American League of Lobbyists), seminars
  offered by, 165–166

allies
  congressional members, 102–103
  cultivating, 15, 163
  documenting in resource book, 18
  ensuring effectiveness of, 163
  establishing ground rules for, 15–16
  in government agencies, 99–101
  identifying, 14–16
  obtaining endorsements from, 104
  obtaining in private sector, 103
  other interest groups, 101–103
The Almanac of American Politics
  analyzing congressional districts with, 24
  obtaining, 167
  researching voting patterns via, 17
American League of Lobbyists (ALL), seminars
  offered by, 165–166
anger, suppressing, 163
appointments cross-index for Hill blitz, 28, 135–137
Appropriations Committee, 47
arrests, managing for demonstrations, 26
awards, giving as gifts to congressmen and senators, 111–112

B

"bad press," evaluating and managing, 39–41
Bill Status Office, contacting, 181
bills. *See also* laws
  consideration in hearings, 63–64
  keeping up with status of, 171–172, 181

number introduced annually, 78
obtaining copies of, 175–176
opposing in hearings, 65
procedures regarding, 46–47
submitting to subcommittees, 16–17
supporting in hearings, 64–65
tracking via THOMAS, 181
Bipartisan Campaign Reform Act, 105–106, 108
blitz. *See* Hill blitz
blogs, accessing, 182
books
giving as gifts to politicians, 109, 111
on lobbying, 186–187
breach of confidence, impact of, 35–36
briefing papers
collaborating with congressional staff members
on, 94–95
preparation of, 78
Brookings Institute, seminars offered by, 165
"bruised ego" syndrome, 148
Bureau of National Affairs, obtaining newsletters
by, 172

C
cab system in D.C., 185–186
calendar, developing for Hill blitz, 135–137
Campaign & Elections political blog directory, 182
campaign committees, making donations to, 114
campaign contributions. *See also* contributions;
gift categories; money
consulting with campaign treasurer about, 114
handling by political action committees, 109
prohibition on giving cash, 114–116
regulation of, 113–114
reporting and documenting accurately,
116–117
candidates
contribution limits for, 110
deciding on support of, 118–119
making donations to, 114
meeting at fundraisers, 124
Capitol Switchboard, contacting, 181
cash, prohibition in gift-giving, 114–116
catalog of U.S. government publications, obtaining,
171
caucuses
number of, 178
obtaining analyses by, 178–179
celebrity speakers
inviting to demonstrations, 56–57
testimony at congressional hearings, 66
CFR (*Code of Federal Regulations*), obtaining, 177

changed circumstances, impact on lobbying campaigns, 145–146
charity events, 113
clearance procedures in action plan, 22–23
clerk of the House of Representatives
contacting, 170
reporting lobbying activities to, 4–5, 106,
107
clipping services, 38–39, 182–183
Cloak Rooms, contacting, 181
Code of Federal Regulations (CFR), obtaining,
177
columnists, interacting with, 36–37
committee and subcommittee members
categorizing by access, 17
contacting, 17
determining voting patterns of, 17
number of, 46
writing letters to, 46
committees and subcommittees
obtaining reports from, 175
scheduling hearings before, 64–65
staffs of, 86–87
submitting bills to, 16–17
community relations, considering in demonstrations, 61
compromise, importance of, 15
confrontations, avoiding with other special interest
groups, 102
congressional contacts
creating preliminary list of, 16–17
documenting in action plan, 23–24
documenting in resource book, 19
Congressional Directory
identifying committee and subcommittee
members via, 17
obtaining, 166
congressional fundraisers. *See* fundraisers (congressional)
congressional hearings
answering questions in, 69–70
getting invited to, 65–66
making statements in, 66–67
obtaining information about, 175
planting questions in, 68–69
presenting views in, 66–67
press coverage of, 70–71
record taken of, 71
scheduling, 64–65
significance of, 63–64
congressional members. *See* members of Congress
Congressional Quarterly, subscribing to, 171

Congressional Record
  being included in, 74
  consulting, 174
  errors in, 145
  importance to lobbyists, 73–74
  reprinting of remarks from, 74–75
  role in congressional hearings, 71–73
congressional staff counsel, meeting with, 87
Congressional Staff Directory, obtaining, 166
congressional staff members
  AAs (administrative assistants), 79–81
  being considerate of, 148–149
  briefing prior to meetings, 94–95
  committee staffs, 86–87
  importance of, 77
  including in lobbying campaigns, 148–149
  initial contact with personal staff, 87–88
  interacting with, 149
  job demands of, 78
  LAs (legislative assistants), 85–86
  lunch meetings with, 88–89
  number of, 77
  personal secretaries, 81–82
  press aides, 83–85
congressional staff system, structure of, 78–79
congressional visits
  appropriate behavior for, 96
  arranging, 94
  attending and conducting, 95–96
  following up on, 97–98
  planning, 91–92
  staying focused in, 96
  taking notes during, 96
Congressional Yellow Book
  identifying committee and subcommittee
    members via, 17
  obtaining, 167
Congressional ZIP Code Directory, obtaining, 170
congressmen. *See* members of Congress
consultants, hiring to target potential contributors,
  121
contacts, planning, coordinating, and following up
  on, 162
contributions. *See also* campaign contributions; gift
    categories; money
  guidelines for, 118–119
  law related to, 108–109, 110
  nonpolitical, 117–118
control number, including on resource book, 19
credibility
  enhancing, 14–15
  retaining, 14, 141

D
"dear colleague" letters, writing, 102–103
delivery services, 183–184
demonstrations
  appealing to justice in, 59
  avoiding zealotry in, 59–60
  community relations for, 61
  dealing with police agencies for, 60
  designing symbols and signs for, 57–58
  documenting in action plan, 25–26
  effectiveness of, 55
  estimating numbers of, 57
  getting housing for, 62
  getting permits for, 62
  versus Hill blitzes, 134
  inviting celebrity speakers to, 56–57
  logistics of, 61–62
  planning, 55–56
  planning transportation for, 62
  scheduling, 58–59
  timing of, 58–59
  weather considerations, 58
district maps, documenting in action plan, 24
donations. *See* contributions

E
editors, approaching, 31
egos, bruised, 148
e-mail
  letter-writing campaigns via, 53–54
  press releases via, 38
  sending to congressional staff members, 88
endorsements, obtaining from allies, 104
errata sheets, distributing, 144
errors
  correcting immediately, 162
  of fact, avoiding, 141
  recovering from, 144–145
Ethics Committees, significance of, 112
"exclusive" interviews, granting, 35
executive branch. *See* administrative agencies
expenditures, documenting, 116

F
fact checking, importance of, 142
fact sheets, using in letter-writing campaigns,
  48–51
facts
  knowing and expressing accurately, 161
  recovering from misstatement of, 144–145
fanaticism, avoiding, 59–60, 163
Federal Election Campaign Act, 105–106, 108–109

Federal Election Commission (FEC)
  information on campaign contributions from,
    109, 110
  reporting fundraising activities to, 119–120
Federal Register, consulting, 174
Federal Regulation of Lobbying Act, 4–5,
    105–106
Federal Yellow Book, obtaining, 168
finances, analyzing, 118
527 organizations, third-party fundraising by,
    120–121
floor information, obtaining, 181
Foreign Agents Registration Act, 5
foreign interests, lobbyists working on behalf of, 5
form letters, treatment of, 47–48. See also letters
fundraisers (congressional)
  accepting invitations to, 122–123
  arriving at, 123
  circulating at, 124–125
  consuming liquor and food at, 123
  following up on, 125–126
  getting invited to, 122
  maximizing benefits of, 126
  socializing with other lobbyists at, 125
fundraising, 119–121
  sample letter for, 119–120
  third-party, 120–121
funds, managing, 118–119

G
gift categories. See also campaign contributions;
    contributions; money
  awards, 111
  books, 109, 111
  charity events, 113
  gifts under five dollars, 111
  liquor, 111–112
  models and samples, 112
gimmicks
  attracting media attention with, 27
  avoiding disruptive gimmicks, 126–127
  contacting media about, 128–130
  keeping cheap, 130
  keeping relevant to issues, 126
  successful examples of, 130–131
  visibility of, 128
"good press," explanation of, 33–34
government agencies. See administrative agencies
governmental material
  bills and committee prints, 175–176
  Code of Federal Regulations (CFR), 177
  Congressional Record, 174

Federal Register, 174
  hearings and reports, 175
  KnowLegis, 180
  special interest caucus and study committee
    analyses, 178–179
  THOMAS, 174
  United States Code, 176–177
  whip notices, 179–180
Greater Washington Board of Trade, contacting, 186

H
hearings. See congressional hearings
Hill blitz
  appointments cross-index for, 28, 135
  assessing supporters after, 139
  assigning teams to, 134
  constituent-relations aspect of, 133
  coordinating, 137–138
  versus demonstrating, 133
  developing calendar for, 136–137
  documenting in action plan, 27–28
  explanation of, 133
  following up on, 139
  lead time for, 133
  meetings related to, 138–139
  rehearsing for, 139
  scheduling teams for meetings related to, 135
  setting up appointments for, 134–137
  using interview sheets in, 137
hostile press, responding to, 40–41
hotels in D.C., 184
House floor information, obtaining, 181
House Rules Committee, significance of, 17
housing, planning for demonstrations, 62
Hudson's Washington News Media Contacts
    Directory
  identifying press contacts via, 22
  obtaining, 169
humor, importance of, 164

I
informants, advisory about use of, 14
information, providing on request, 141–142
insults
  cultivating immunity to, 164
  occurrence of, 146–148
integrity, importance of, 14
interest groups. See special interest groups
interview sheets
  importance of, 138
  reviewing, 138–139
  using in Hill blitz, 137

interviews, granting "exclusive," 35
issues
 anticipating questions related to, 11–12
 documenting in resource book, 19
 focusing on, 14
 identifying for lobbying, 9

J
journalists. *See* reporters
justice, appealing to in demonstrations, 59

K
Kiplinger Letter, subscribing to, 172
KnowLegis, online service of, 180

L
LAs. *See* legislative assistants
law firms
 in D.C., 154
 discovering lobbying history of, 156
 discussing payment of, 157
 obtaining professional lawyer-lobbyists from,
  154–155
 requesting proposal for lawyer-lobbyists from,
  157
laws. *See also* bills
 being knowledgeable about, 16
 Bipartisan Campaign Reform Act, 105–106,
  108
 determining current status of, 16
 documenting in resource book, 18
 Federal Election Campaign Act, 105–106,
  108–109
 Federal Regulation of Lobbying Act, 4–5,
  105–106
 Foreign Agents Registration Act, 5
 Lobbying Disclosure Act, 105–108
 related to lobbying, 4–5, 105–106
legal advice, importance to lobbying campaigns, 16
legal directories, Web site for, 153
legal memoranda
 documenting in resource book, 18
 requesting from law firms, 16
legislation. *See* bills
legislation enforcement, identifying administrative
  agencies related to, 17
legislative assistants (LAs)
 interacting with, 85–86
 keeping informed, 148
 roles and responsibilities of, 85
legislative hearings, significance of, 63
legislative process, being familiar with, 163–164

letter-writing campaigns
 following up on responses to, 51–53
 format and content of letters in, 44
 importance of spontaneity in, 48
 organizing, 45–46
 personalizing letters in, 47
 recommended length of letters in, 43–44
 sample letter for, 44–45
 using fact sheets in, 48–51
letters. *See also* form letters; letter-writing campaigns
 for accepting invitations to fundraisers, 122
 documenting in action plan, 24
 to the editor, 40–41
 for fundraising, 119–120
 including with fact sheets, 50–51
 including with personal-check contributions,
  115
 sending after attending fundraisers, 125
 sending as follow-up to congressional visits,
  97–98
 writing "dear colleague" letters, 102–103
 writing thank-you letters after Hill blitzes, 139
liquor, giving as gifts to congressmen and senators,
  111–112
lobbies
 multiple-issue lobbies, 8–9
 single-issue lobbies, 7–8
lobbying. *See also* Ten Commandments of
   Lobbying
 books on, 186–187
 controversy around definition of, 4
 versus demonstrating, 55
 history of, 2–4
 institutionalization of, 2
 laws related to, 4–5, 105–106
 objective of, 16
 original secrecy around, 3
 relevance to American political system, 5–6
lobbying campaigns
 adjusting based on feedback from letters, 51–52
 foundation of, 91
 identifying target members for, 16
 impact of changed circumstances on, 145–146
 importance of legal advice to, 16
Lobbying Disclosure Act, 105–108
lobbying firms, obtaining professional lobbyists
  from, 158–159
lobbyists. *See also* professional lobbyists
 disclosure of activities, 4
 information required of, 107–108
 laws of relevance to, 4–5, 105–106

registration of, 106
regulations related to foreign interests, 5
responsibilities of, 106–107
log rolling, 103
lunch meetings with congressional staff members, 88–89

M

marshals, employing for demonstrations, 25–26
Martindale-Hubbell, Web site for, 153
McCain-Feingold Act. *See* Bipartisan Campaign Reform Act
media. *See also* press releases; reporters
answering inquiries from, 23
attracting attention from, 27, 31–32, 56, 128
"bad press," 39–41
contacting, 34–36, 128–130
coverage of congressional hearings by, 65, 70–71
documenting in action plan, 21–23
enhancing relations with, 31–32
"good press," 33–34
opinion columns, 36–37
putting in touch with press aides, 84–85
members of Congress
allying with, 102–103
definition of, 2
gifts to, 109–113
identifying target members, 16
lobbying devices of, 102–103
number of, 46
obtaining information about, 167
personal staff of, 79
preparing summary sheets about, 92–94
protecting from unethical conduct, 112
referring to by titles, 148
tracking with KnowLegis, 180
memorandum of understanding, drafting for other special interest groups, 101–102
messenger services, 183–184
Metro public transportation system, 185
mistakes. *See* errors
models, giving as gifts to congressmen and senators, 112
money. *See also* campaign contributions; contributions; fundraising; gift categories
being frugal with, 164
regulations on raising and spending of, 105–109
multiple-issue lobbies, power of, 8–9

N

National Journal, subscribing to, 171–172
national parties, contribution limits for, 110
networks. *See* media
news media. *See* media
newsletters
from Bureau of National Affairs, 172
from Kiplinger, 172
from members of Congress, 84
newspapers, subscribing to, 173–174
nonpolitical contributions, 117–118

O

office space, 186
opinion columns, 36–37
opposition
documenting in resource book, 18
identifying, 13–14, 161–162
oversight hearings, significance of, 63–64

P

PACs. *See* political action committees
panels of witnesses at congressional hearings, 67–68
party organizations, gaining access to, 103
periodicals
Bureau of National Affairs newsletters, 172
Congressional Quarterly, 171
Kiplinger Letter, 172
National Journal, 171–172
newspapers, 173–174
by trade associations and interest groups, 173
permits, getting for demonstrations, 62
personal checks, giving as campaign contributions, 115–116
personal secretaries
interacting with, 82
roles and responsibilities of, 81–82
personal staffs. *See* congressional staff members
pocket manuals, obtaining, 169
police agencies, dealing with in demonstrations, 60
political action committees (PACs)
establishing, 109
fundraising via, 119–120
handling of donations by, 109–110
political blogs, accessing, 182
political campaigns, making contributions to, 109
political candidates. *See* candidates
political system, relevance of lobbying to, 5–6
political versus nonpolitical expenditures, 117

politicians. *See* candidates; members of Congress

press. *See* media

press aides
  interacting with, 84–85
  keeping informed, 148
  roles and responsibilities of, 83

press releases
  clearing and delivering, 38
  contents of, 37–38
  determining effect of, 38–39
  distributing for demonstrations, 57
  documenting in action plan, 22–23
  example of, 83–84
  issuing for congressional hearing appearances,
    70–71

press services, working with, 183

private sector, making allies in, 103

professional lobbyists. *See also* lobbyists
  capabilities of, 151–152
  choosing, 153
  costs of, 152–153, 157
  interviewing, 155–157
  versus lawyers, 151
  obtaining from law firms, 154
  obtaining from public relations firms, 157–158

promises, keeping, 15

proposals from other groups, responding to, 15

public relations firms, obtaining professional lob-
    byists from, 157–158

publishers, approaching, 31

Q

questions
  answering in congressional hearings, 69–70
  documenting "party line" answers in resource
    book, 19
  planting in congressional hearings, 68–69
  researching answers to, 11–12
  specifying contact persons to answer in action
    plan, 22–23

R

radio, contacting about gimmicks, 129–130

the *Record. See Congressional Record*

reference manuals
  The Almanac of American Politics, 167
  catalog of U.S. government publications, 171
  Congressional Directory, 166
  Congressional Staff Directory, 166
  Congressional Yellow Book, 167

  Congressional ZIP Code Directory, 170
  Federal Yellow Book, 168
  *Hudson's Washington News Media Contacts
    Directory*, 169
  pocket manuals, 169
  Rules of the House of Representatives, 170
  Standing Rules of the Senate, 170
  Washington Representatives, 168

releases. *See* press releases

reporters. *See also* media
  approaching, 31, 34–35
  documenting in action plan, 22
  encountering hostility from, 33
  establishing ground rules with, 35
  "good guys" versus "bad guys," 33
  talking to, 32–33

reporting sheet, including with PAC fundraising
    letter, 120

resource book
  confidentiality of, 19
  contents of, 18–19
  importance of, 20

restaurants in D.C., 184–185

revenue measures, committees related to, 46–47

Rules Committee, 46

Rules of the House of Representatives, obtaining, 170

S

samples, giving as gifts to congressmen and sena-
    tors, 112

secretary of the Senate
  contacting, 170
  reporting lobbying activities to, 106, 107

security, providing for demonstrations, 25–26

seminars, 165–166

Senate floor information, obtaining, 181

senators. *See* members of Congress

setbacks, overcoming, 164

signs and symbols, designing for demonstrations,
    57–58

single-issue lobbies, impact on public policy, 7–8

single-issue political goals, impossibility of, 9

sources, credibility of, 142

special interest caucuses, obtaining analyses by,
    178–179

special interest groups
  as allies, 14–16, 101–103
  avoiding confrontations with, 102
  effectiveness of, 7–8
  obtaining listings of, 168

obtaining ratings of congressional members by, 167

as opponents, 13–14

periodicals published by, 173

stigma associated with, 5–6

writing memorandum of understanding for, 101–102

staff counsel, meeting with, 87

staff members. *See* congressional staff members

Standing Rules of the Senate, obtaining, 170

statements

having printed in *Congressional Record*, 71

providing in congressional hearings, 66–67

reviewing others' statements prior to hearings, 67

statistics, presenting, 142–143

stenographers, use at congressional hearings, 71

study committees, analyses conducted by, 178–179

subcommittee members. *See* committee and subcommittee members

subcommittees. *See* committees and subcommittees

summary sheet, preparing for congressmen and senators, 92–94

supporters. *See* allies

swing members, visiting, 91

symbols and signs, designing for demonstrations, 57–58

T

target members, identifying, 16

taxis in D.C., 185

television stations, contacting about gimmicks, 128–129

Ten Commandments of Lobbying. *See also* lobbying

Avoid Zealotry, 163

Be Frugal with Your Money, 164

Correct Errors Immediately, 162

Cultivate Your Allies, 163

Grow Thick Skin, 164

Know the Legislative Process, 163–164

Know Your Facts and Be Accurate in Expressing Them, 161

Know Your Opposition, 161–162

Plan, Coordinate, and Follow Up on Each Contact, 162

Win, 164

testimony, providing at congressional hearings, 66–67

thank-you letters

sending after congressional visits, 97–98

writing after Hill blitzes, 139

third-party fundraisers, holding, 120–121

THOMAS

consulting, 174

identifying committee and subcommittee members via, 17

obtaining bills from, 176

tracking bills through, 181

trade associations, periodicals published by, 173

training programs. *See* seminars

transcripts, receiving for congressional hearings, 71

transportation

Metro public transportation system, 185

providing for demonstrations, 26, 62

taxis, 185–186

U

United States Code, obtaining, 176–177

V

vote listings on legislation, accessing, 74

voting patterns, researching for committee members, 17

voting records, obtaining for congressional members, 167

W

Washington Representatives, obtaining, 168

weather, considering in planning demonstrations, 58

whip notices, publication of, 179–180

whips, contact information for, 180

winning, focusing on, 164

witness panels at congressional hearings, 67–68

witness statements. *See* statements

Z

zealotry, avoiding, 59–60, 163

ZIP code database, accessing, 170